War and British society
1688–1815

New Studies in Economic and Social History

Edited for the Economic History Society by
Michael Sanderson
University of East Anglia, Norwich

This series, specially commissioned by the Economic History Society, provides a guide to the current interpretations of the key themes of economic and social history in which advances have recently been made or in which there has been significant debate.

In recent times economic and social history has been one of the most flourishing areas of historical study. This has mirrored the increasing relevance of the economic and social sciences both in a student's choice of career and in forming a society at large more aware of the importance of these issues in their everyday lives. Moreover specialist interests in business, agricultural and welfare history, for example, have themselves burgeoned and there has been an increased interest in the economic development of the wider world. Stimulating as these scholarly developments have been for the specialist, the rapid advance of the subject and the quantity of new publications make it difficult for the reader to gain an overview of particular topics, let alone the whole field.

New Studies in Economic and Social History is intended for students and their teachers. It is designed to introduce them to fresh topics and to enable them to keep abreast of recent writing and debates. All the books in the series are written by a recognised authority in the subject, and the arguments and issues are set out in a critical but unpartisan fashion. The aim of the series is to survey the current state of scholarship, rather than to provide a set of pre-packaged conclusions.

The series has been edited since its inception in 1968 by Professors M. W. Flinn, T. C. Smout and L. A. Clarkson, and is currently edited by Dr Michael Sanderson. From 1968 it was published by Macmillan as *Studies in Economic History*, and after 1974 as *Studies in Economic and Social History*. From 1995 *New Studies in Economic and Social History* is being published on behalf of the Economic History Society by Cambridge University Press. This new series includes some of the titles previously published by Macmillan as well as new titles, and reflects the ongoing development throughout the world of this rich seam of history.

For a full list of titles in print, please see the end of the book.

War and British society
1688–1815

Prepared for the Economic History Society by

H. V. Bowen

CAMBRIDGE
UNIVERSITY PRESS

CAMBRIDGE UNIVERSITY PRESS
Cambridge, New York, Melbourne, Madrid, Cape Town,
Singapore, São Paulo, Delhi, Mexico City

Cambridge University Press
The Edinburgh Building, Cambridge CB2 8RU, UK

Published in the United States of America by Cambridge University Press, New York

www.cambridge.org
Information on this title: www.cambridge.org/9780521576451

First published 1998

A catalogue record for this publication is available from the British Library

Library of Congress Cataloguing in Publication Data

Bowen, H.V.
War and British Society, 1688–1815/prepared
for the Economic History Society by H.V. Bowen.
   p.   cm. – (New studies in economic and social history)
Includes biographical references and index.
ISBN 0 521 57226 6 (hc). – ISBN 0 521 57645 8 (pbk)
1. Great Britain – History, Military – 18th century.
2. Great Britain – Social conditions – 18th century.
3. Social change – Great Britain – History.
I. Economic History Society. II. Title. III. Series.
DA67.B69 1998
941–dc21
97-42249 CIP

ISBN 978-0-521-57226-2 Hardback
ISBN 978-0-521-57645-1 Paperback

Contents

Acknowledgements

I am indebted to Philip Cottrell, Peter D. G. Thomas, David M. Williams and Nuala Zahedieh for their close reading and helpful criticisms of an early draft of this booklet. In addition, the series editor, Michael Sanderson, made some important suggestions, for which I am grateful. Of course, I alone bear responsibility for any remaining errors, omissions, or shortcomings. I must also thank Patrick O'Brien for discussing with me the problems and pitfalls in writing on this subject, and for supplying me with copies of inaccessible published items.

1
Introduction

Historical explorations of the effects of war upon Britain's society and economy have focused, for the most part, on the twentieth century. This is not surprising in view of the profound effect that two world wars have had upon patterns of economic and social change, and considerable attention has been paid by historians to the ways in which those wars and their legacy helped to shape or reshape the contours of modern British society. As a result, a rich and detailed literature sheds light upon almost every conceivable aspect of the British domestic experience during the age of 'total' warfare. Although important, a concentration on the twentieth century can be misplaced, however, because war also exerted considerable influence over the earlier development of Britain's society and economy. This was especially so during the 'long eighteenth century' – from 1688 to 1815 – when Britain was at war for much of the time and contemporaries still adhered to the fatalistic belief that war, if not ever present in their lives, was always to be expected (Ceadel, 1996: 4–5).

The importance of war during the eighteenth century has, of course, long been recognised by historians. Over a hundred years ago, Sir John Seeley was moved to comment that war was the 'characteristic feature' of the period, while more recently the eighteenth century has been described as an 'age of war' (Seeley, 1883: 25; Langford, 1976: 23). Yet, although warfare provides, as Seeley noted, some of the most important basic punctuation marks in eighteenth-century British history, the study of war itself long remained primarily the preserve of military and diplomatic historians. They confined their attention to the battlefield or naval engagement and only over the last few decades have the wider economic and social influences of warfare been fully acknowledged and examined. As historians working in quite different areas of endeavour have explored the domestic dimension of eighteenth-century great-power conflicts, so the centrality of war in the development of Britain's economy and society has become increasingly more apparent. Even so, although much recent progress has been made, a great deal of scholarly work remains to be undertaken in this field of study, and many of the domestic economic and social effects of the major wars of the period remain unexplored. In particular, with the notable exception of the War of Spanish Succession (Jones, 1989), none of the international conflicts of the first three-quarters of the eighteenth century has been studied in anything like the same depth as Britain's struggle against Revolutionary and Napoleonic France. This means that the wars of 1793 to 1815 tend to provide most of the detailed case studies for those seeking to explore the nature of the relationship between war and economic and social change. As a result of this marked imbalance in the historiography of the subject, general conclusions about the domestic effects of war across the whole of the long eighteenth century must remain, at best, tentative and provisional.

In spite of these words of caution, it cannot be denied that all aspects of life in Britain were touched by war during a century and a quarter when a wide range of economic and social institutions, processes, and structures were transformed. Yet the part played by international conflict in facilitating these domestic transformations was not always apparent to contemporaries who, for the most part, viewed the consequences of war as disastrous. Quite understandably, they formed this view on the basis of their assessment of the short-term destructive impact of war, which manifested itself to them most obviously in heavy financial, human and material losses. Historians, on the other hand, have been able to adopt a long-term perspective on the wars of the eighteenth century, and this has enabled them to identify several creative war-related influences at work within Britain's economy and society. Gradually, for example, four distinct nations – England, Scotland, Wales and, after 1800, Ireland – were unified under one crown and parliament, and the authority of this new polity was reinforced by a sense of common identity which transcended long-standing regional and local loyalties, and was sharpened by the experience of war. The strength of this emergent 'British' nation was bolstered in an institutional sense by the development of reasonably effective state and government machinery, designed with the primary aim of mobilising unprecedented levels of manpower and financial resources for war. Finally, of course, the economy and society that supported and sustained Britain's war efforts against rival powers was slowly and fitfully transformed by the various processes associated with industrialisation. Indeed, the early years of the classically formulated 'Industrial Revolution' are to be found in the second half of this period, when Britain was at war for much of the time.

In each of these major areas of development – nation, state, society and economy – war has been identified as a powerful agent of change; but it is important that war is not simply seen as having had a catalytic effect upon Britain's economy and society, remorselessly facilitating improvement, innovation and modernisation. First and foremost, as contemporaries recognised, war was extremely disruptive, and this ensured that lines of development were never straight and unbroken. It is necessary, therefore, to acknowledge the importance of deviations from long-run economic and social trends caused, directly and indirectly, by the great-power struggle. Yet the number of transitions from peace to war, and war to peace, was such that it has not been easy for historians firmly to establish what 'normal' economic and social conditions were during the eighteenth century. Indeed, from 1739 the frequency of war was such that periods of peace could almost be regarded as exceptions to the wartime norm. This immediately calls into question any analytical approach to the period which, as with historians of the twentieth century, regards major wars as abnormal events quickening the long-term socio-economic trends evident in peacetime or, alternatively, causing the development of entirely new forms of economic and social organisation. Circumstances were so very different during the eighteenth century, with war being a semi-permanent feature on the historical landscape, that another set of general questions offer themselves for consideration. How, for example, did the British state manage to sustain its military performance for a century and a quarter? To what extent was Britain's economy and society geared to war throughout the period? Did Britain become a military state? And was Britain's development as an industrial nation assisted or damaged by war?

Finally, these introductory remarks must conclude with the reminder that, in addition to war, other powerful influences helped to effect the transformation of Britain into the world's leading commercial, imperial, industrial and military power by 1815. To ignore population growth, changing patterns of demand, improvements in agriculture, trade and transport, and the advance of science and technology is to ignore circumstances in which economic and social changes often manifest themselves in outcomes that are dependent upon the interaction of many different factors. The isolation of war from those other factors does scant justice to the complexities of the historical process. Nevertheless, in spite of this important *caveat*, it is the direct and indirect influences of war, and the relationship between short- and long-term war-induced economic and social changes, that lie at the heart of this book. Consequently, the chapters that follow might each be taken to represent a test of Heraclitus' famous maxim that 'war is the father of all things'. Chapter 1 establishes the broad context for subsequent discussion by examining the assumptions behind, and consequences of, Britain's approach to war. Chapter 2 looks at how the state coped with the demands of war. Chapter 3 examines the effects of war upon British society, and chapter 4 considers the economic impact of war.

2
Eighteenth-century warfare: the British experience

Between 1688 and 1815 England, or (after 1707) Britain, participated in seven major international wars in Europe and the wider world. Such was the recurrent and sustained nature of conflict with France and Spain that some modern historians have used the term the 'Second Hundred Years War' to describe the period (Meyer and Bromley, 1980), even if this is inaccurate in view of a lengthy period of Anglo-French co-operation between 1716 and 1730 (Black, 1985: 1–12). Nevertheless, as D. B. Horn, the diplomatic historian, once observed, the peace treaties of the eighteenth century represented little more than 'mere truces' in the on-going struggle for supremacy being waged between Britain and France (quoted in Emsley, 1979: 4). This comment echoes the prediction made by Pitt the Elder in 1763 that the Peace of Paris would be an 'armed truce only' (Simmons and Thomas, 1982, I: 441). Pitt was grinding a political axe when he made this remark, but he was acknowledging that all periods of eighteenth-century peace were uneasy times, when finances were repaired and military losses made good in readiness for the next, inevitable conflict.

During these years of war and peace Britain's status and standing among the European powers was not only transformed, but its overseas empire, trade, and commerce expanded. Much to the surprise of many contemporaries, and in spite of serious setbacks such as the loss of the North American colonies in 1783, British forces secured victories on land and sea that enhanced Britain's reputation in Europe and led to its steady ascendancy through the ranks of the great powers. The rather undistinguished military record of the seventeenth century faded from memory as Britain traded blow for blow against its European enemies throughout the eighteenth century. In the ultimate, titanic, struggle against Napoleonic France, the British state, with assistance from its allies, demonstrated that it had developed the capacity, stamina, resources and will to overcome all challengers.

A century and a quarter of conflict opened with the Nine Years' War (1689–97), soon followed by the War of Spanish Succession (1702–13). Then, in turn, came the Wars of Jenkins's Ear and Austrian Succession (1739–48), the Seven Years' War (1756–63), and the War of American Independence (1775–83), before British hegemony was finally established during wars with Revolutionary and Napoleonic France (1793–1801 and 1803–15). These conflicts, which were manifestations of a developing long-term struggle among the European powers for security, commercial advantage and imperial ascendancy, lasted for sixty-five years and thus meant that Britain was engaged in major hostilities for almost exactly half of the period under review. But such a simple calculation does not reveal the full extent to which Britain was involved in war during the course of the long eighteenth century. Many of the years commonly placed by modern historians within periods of 'peace' were characterised by considerable military and naval activity both within Europe and further afield. For example, the longest period of sustained peace for Britain is usually held to be from the signing of the Treaty of Utrecht in 1713 to the outbreak of the War of Jenkins's Ear in 1739. Yet during this quarter century Britain took a leading part in the War of the Quadruple Alliance against Spain (1718–20), fought a minor undeclared war of its own against the same enemy in 1727, and conducted extensive naval operations against Sweden between 1715 and 1717. Closer to home, the authorities had to put down the Jacobite rising in Scotland in 1715 and had to fend off an attempted Spanish–Jacobite invasion in 1719. Later, responding to the threat posed by Spanish-backed former slaves on the island of Jamaica, a small number of troops were sent to assist the planter community during the first Maroon War (1730–9). This pattern was subsequently repeated several times during the course of the century, and all periods of formal peace between the great powers were punctuated by colonial wars, diplomatic crises, naval skirmishes, mobilisations and war scares. Accordingly, there were very few years when British forces were not engaged in military or naval action of one sort or another somewhere in the world. The combined weight of these different types of formal and informal warfare meant that, at any given time, Britain was either actively engaged in war, making preparations for war, or seeking to recover from extended military conflict.

Strategic policy and the British way in war

If the frequency of armed conflict represented one of the main features of the eighteenth century, then the changing nature of war and the conduct of warfare marked another. Indeed, historians have argued that the unprecedented geographical range of the Seven Years' War was such that, as Winston Churchill once remarked, it should properly be regarded as the 'first world war' (Kennedy, 1976: 98–107). At the same time, attempts have been made to discern the defining characteristics of 'modern war' in the military struggles of the late eighteenth and early nineteenth centuries. Recent discussion has been characterised by debate about the long-run nature of the changes that were taking place in military organisation, strategy and weaponry. It used to be held that such changes led to a 'Military Revolution' in Europe between 1560 and 1660 (Roberts, 1956). In recent years, however, historians have questioned this concept of a revolution by drawing attention to the way in which a series of important developments occurred from the middle of the fifteenth century right through to the end of the eighteenth century (Parker, 1988; Black, 1991, 1994a and 1994b). As part of this broad-ranging discussion of the transformation of the way in which warfare was conducted, it has often been argued that by the second half of the eighteenth century a new all-embracing type of warfare was evolving which drew whole societies and economies, as well as armies and navies, into the conflict between the great powers. The French Wars (1793–1815) are usually held to have marked the emergence of this recognisably modern form of war by incorporating central features such as the mass mobilisation of adult males, the systematic use of 'economic' warfare and financial attrition to defeat enemies, and unprecedented levels of organisation and regulation of the civilian population.

Recently, however, renewed discussion about the timing of some of these important developments in warfare has been prompted by the claim that the War of American Independence and not the French Wars of 1793 to 1815 might properly be regarded as the first war of a modern type. This is because it is held to have marked a significant departure from the 'limited' conflicts staged between European states during the earlier part of the century (Conway, 1995a; 1995b: 23–42). Far from being limited in scope or having little economic and social impact upon life in Britain, it has been argued that the American War 'anticipated in many important ways the British experience in the French Revolutionary War' (Conway, 1995a: 127). Indeed, as Conway puts it, the war for America was 'the first war of the new order' (Conway, 1995b: 23). Whatever the merits of this particular case, and they are a matter for debate, it is important that changes in the conduct of warfare during the final quarter of the eighteenth century should not obscure the fact that from 1688 every major war between the European powers quickened the processes which served to broaden and deepen the conduct of military conflict between nations (Black, 1994b). Wars were broadened in the sense that they became increasingly global in scope as conflict on the Continent spilled over into colonial and other extra-European spheres of activity. At the same time, the nature of conflict deepened as wars absorbed ever-greater levels of human, financial and material resources. Because of this, the effect that warfare had upon societies and economies throughout Europe became progressively more marked, and there is much strength in the argument that the wars of the period between 1775 and 1815 marked a logical extension of, rather than a radical departure from, what had gone before (French, 1990: 62).

With regard to Britain, these general trends in the conduct of eighteenth-century warfare were reflected in a number of different ways. At the most basic of levels, technological developments caused significant alterations in the ways that the army and navy organised themselves and fought in battle. As far as the army was concerned, for example, new weaponry in the form of the flintlock musket and the socket bayonet rendered pikes obsolete, heralding the emergence of the general infantryman during the early years of the eighteenth century (Black, 1994b: 38–41). Shortly afterwards, technological advances in gunnery led to the establishment of artillery and engineer companies, or 'Scientific Corps' as they were known. This was a development which represented an acknowledgement that some tasks were now best performed by specialised trained units. At sea, the introduction of the highly effective fast-firing carronade to some of the navy's ships during the last decades of the eighteenth century prompted a move away from tactics based upon lines of battle which had hitherto dominated naval thinking. This played an important part in enabling the Royal Navy to inflict heavy losses upon French warships during the Revolutionary and Napoleonic Wars (Kennedy, 1976: 126–7).

Change was also reflected in the way that European warfare was increasingly conducted beyond the Continent (Black, 1994b: 1–37). In part, this stemmed from the development after 1650 of a British strategy founded upon naval power. In addition to the defence of home waters and the all-important blockade of enemy ports, pressure was applied in far-flung corners of the world as a means of weakening rival powers such as France and Spain. A recent formulation has, however, described this as a 'blue water' policy embodying much more than simply the use of the navy in the wider world. In part, this was because the effective use of sea power had a considerable bearing upon the situation in Europe where Britain had several key commercial and strategic interests requiring naval protection (Baugh, 1988a; Kennedy, 1976: 86–94). Yet Britain could not afford to turn its back on land-based European theatres of war because France could never be defeated by seapower alone. Indeed, it has recently been argued that the lack of effective strategy ensured that the navy was not a 'decisive instrument of power' until the Seven Years' War (Jones, 1988: 47). Instead, as an extension of a 'continental' strategy based upon land and amphibious operations fought alongside allies in Europe, aggressive overseas actions together with the command of European waters were deliberately and consistently brought to bear upon the general military and diplomatic situation (French, 1990).

The application of this strategy in a major conflict occurred first during the 1690s when England undertook what has been described as a 'double forward commitment' involving the simultaneous mobilisation and deployment of the army and the navy (Jones, 1989: 16). This approach to war was designed primarily to influence the outcome of hostilities between the major powers in Europe. Over time, however, Britain was also able to use it to protect its burgeoning overseas empire and commercial interests. Although contemporaries always eschewed conquest and the pursuit of expansionist policies because they were costly and dangerous, they nevertheless regarded military action against rival local and European powers in the Caribbean, North America and India as vital for the preservation and enhancement of the nation's pride, strength and wealth. The consequences of this global approach to strategy were realised in the peace treaties and settlements that brought European wars to a conclusion, and, beginning with the Treaty of Utrecht, colonial and commercial prizes regularly fell into British hands. When the Treaty of Paris was signed in 1763, none could doubt that Britain's position of ascendancy (although, in the event, short lived) was based in large part upon a willingness to deploy significant wartime resources to the periphery of its empire and to the sea lanes that kept its overseas possessions supplied and protected. British policy-makers increasingly perceived their nation's interests and strategy in global terms and for the most part acted accordingly. The results of this were to be seen in an ever-lengthening list of territories, islands and overseas outposts brought under British control. Indeed, the final conflicts of the period, against Revolutionary and Napoleonic France, helped Britain to enter what has been described as a 'new imperial age' in which extensive gains were made in all parts of the world (Bayly, 1989: 100–32).

By extending military and naval influence across the world, Britain added a new strategic dimension to a long tradition of military endeavour and campaigning in Europe. Although British statesmen no longer had any territorial ambitions in Europe, the prevailing state of the balance of power, and the designs of the French in particular, always served to concentrate their minds on Continental developments. Apart from a brief period of isolation during the 1760s, ministers did not seek to detach themselves from involvement in the diplomatic, political and military affairs of Europe. Although it is possible to argue that 'On balance, decisions [taken by statesmen and diplomats] tended against military commitment on the Continent' (Baugh, 1988a: 34), there were always treaty obligations to uphold and interests to defend in Europe during times of war. This was particularly the case between 1688 and 1760 when the dynastic connections of William III and the first two Georges ensured that Britain maintained close ties with, first, the Dutch Republic and then Hanover. Indeed, the only major war in which Britain failed to deploy troops and resources on the Continent was the War of American Independence, despite the fact that France and Spain intervened on behalf of the colonists after 1777. In other words, Britain's commitment to its navy and increased levels of activity in the wider world were not automatically offset by any reduction of her wartime involvement on mainland Europe. On the contrary, although there was always political opposition to the commitment of troops to the Continent, and although greater financial resources were allocated to the navy than to the army in each war before 1793 (French, 1990: 29, 227), Britain continued to put forces into the field in Europe and to pay large subsidies to its continental allies.

The price of victory: men and money

In terms of the overall structure and distribution of British forces, these strategic considerations had a twofold effect. First, in manpower terms, the wartime navy doubled in size over the century after 1688. Its paper strength reveals that an average annual naval establishment of 40,262 during the Nine Years' War grew to 82,022 by the War of American Independence (Brewer, 1989: 30), and in 1809 the number of seamen and marines touched 130,000 men as the navy attempted to provide crews for an ever-increasing number of vessels (Emsley, 1979: 133). The navy, which possessed 173 ships of all types in 1688, maintained a wartime fleet of between 185 and 350 vessels before 1760. The expansion of the navy during subsequent wars was quite considerable and its number of vessels of all types peaked at 979 in 1809 (Ehrman, 1953: xx; Hattendorf, 1978: 141; Morriss, 1983: 12). This allowed Britain to establish a position of supremacy over the combined fleets of France and Spain during the first half of the eighteenth century. Although this dominance was later eroded, wartime building programmes, and especially the capture and transfer of good quality enemy shipping to the British fleet, eventually enabled the Royal Navy to prevail in the long run over its main rivals (Baugh, 1995: 124–6).

Second, there was also a considerable expansion in the wartime size of the British army, although, as with the navy, numbers were always substantially reduced at the return of peace. Each major war, with the notable exception of the War of Austrian Succession, saw a substantial increase in land forces. This resulted in the average annual size of the army rising from 76,404 men during the Nine Years' War to 108,404 men during the American War (Brewer, 1989: 30), while in 1809, during the Napoleonic War, the number of regular troops and embodied militia increased to over 300,000 men. Seamen, marines, local militia and volunteers took the total number of men in arms to 786,000 in 1809 (Emsley, 1979: 133), and, if colonial troops and the substantial forces of the East India Company are included, it seems clear that by the end of the period Britain was able to match the manpower resources of the European powers. Indeed, if all regular and part-time troops and sailors based at home, in Europe, and across the wider empire are taken into account, it seems likely that Britain had approximately one million men in arms by 1815.

For a number of reasons, most figures related to the size of Britain's armed forces must be treated with a considerable degree of caution. Those for the army are based upon the number of troops voted by Parliament, rather than on the men engaged on active service (Brewer, 1989: 31), and evidence suggests that actual battalion strengths were often considerably less than their authorised establishments (Houlding, 1981: 125–37). Similarly, with respect to the navy, the number of men actually mustered on board ships at any one time was always less than the full complement, or crew strength on paper (Rodger, 1986: 287–8). It must also be borne in mind that a significant proportion of the men included in these figures, especially those relating to the army, were not British subjects, and it has been calculated, for example, that less than half of the 150,000 men in the British army in 1709 were 'subject troops' (Chandler, 1994: 75). This was because throughout the period Parliament authorised the expenditure of large sums of money on the employment of foreign mercenaries during times of war. Although Dutch and German troops were stationed in Britain in 1715–16, 1719, 1744–6, and, most notably, in 1756–7 as attempts were made to counter the threat of invasion (Houlding, 1981: 323), it was often foreign soldiers rather than British subjects who were used in continental theatres of war. In the main, Britons were allocated to home duties and campaigns beyond Europe (Brewer, 1989: 32; Baugh, 1988a: 53–4). Thus, for example, during the 1690s foreign mercenaries represented, as an annual average, around 48 per cent of the English army in Flanders, and by the following decade their share had risen to almost 60 per cent (French, 1990: 10–11). By the Napoleonic War, the proportion of foreign troops in the army had fallen to around a fifth, some 52,000 men (Gates, 1994: 137), but the ranks were instead being swelled with Scottish and Irish soldiers. The number of Scottish troops in the British army grew steadily after 1745, and almost 160,000 Irishmen were incorporated into 'English' regiments at one time or another between 1793 and 1815 (Mokyr 1987: 302). They served to add to the diversity and cosmopolitan nature of those who undertook military service on behalf of the British Crown.

If the presence of foreigners and Irishmen limited the profile of the English, Welsh and, to a lesser degree, Scots within the regular armed forces, the number of Britons experiencing some form of military service was augmented by those who were members of the militia or volunteer corps. The militia, which was reconstituted in 1757 after a lengthy political battle, was organised on a county basis with quotas filled by men chosen by ballot, although the well to do were permitted to pay a fine or provide a substitute in lieu of service. During peacetime, each regiment was supposed to undergo twenty-eight days of training each year, and in wartime units acted both as a defence force and as semi-trained bodies of men upon which the regular army could draw for recruits. The paper strength of the 'new', post-1757, militia rose from 32,000 during the 1760s to over 100,000 in the mid-1790s, when a supplementary Militia Act was passed and quotas were extended to Scotland for the first time (Western, 1965; Beckett, 1991). Not only did this ensure that there was some form of military presence across most of the country at a time when there was widespread fear of invasion but also, over the years, membership of the militia increased the number of men possessing some form of military training, even if only part-time and often very rudimentary (Langford, 1989: 628–9).

This process of military training and organisation was also assisted by the establishment of the volunteer corps and independent companies during the 1790s, when, following the outbreak of the war against France, leading local figures across the country took it upon themselves to raise their own private defence forces. These were similar to the miscellaneous units that had been hastily assembled to repel foreign invasion during the Jacobite rising of 1745 and the American War of Independence (Conway, 1995b: 38), although during the 1790s such companies also had an important additional role to play as counter-revolutionary forces (Western, 1956; Cookson, 1989). By and large, the volunteer forces, in which 100,000 men served between 1793 and 1801 and 400,000 men in 1803–4, pitched their appeal to those whose social background was largely propertied and urban. The volunteers were thus quite different from the labourers who were drafted by ballot into the rank and file of the militia. For the first time, many urban communities were fully mobilised and this meant that, although the volunteer movement faded away after 1804, military service was experienced by a far wider cross-section of the British people than ever before (Colley, 1992: 288–308; Colley, 1994; Cookson, 1989; Western, 1956).

Although it is difficult to estimate with any great accuracy the number of British subjects bearing arms during the wars of the period, it is beyond dispute that, as the nature of warfare changed, there was a marked increase in the proportion of the population who saw military service of one type or another. Very roughly speaking, the 'participation rate' of the men of military age in the armed forces (army, navy, militia and volunteers) increased from 1 in 16 during the War of Austrian Succession to 1 in 10 during the Seven Years' War, to 1 in 8 during the War of American Independence, and finally to 1 in 5 or 6 during the French wars of 1793–1815 (Conway, 1995b: 38; Emsley, 1979: 133). The last figure suggests that by the end of the period between 11 and 14 per cent of the male work force aged between fifteen and forty was recruited into the army and navy (O'Brien, 1989a: 336). Yet the manpower demands of the regular forces, while causing shortages in some areas, do not appear to have caused a general scarcity of labour. The army focused its recruiting energies upon the lower end of the employment scale and, where this served to create gaps in the labour market by drawing unskilled workers into the armed forces, these voids were filled by the unemployed. Only agriculture (Hueckel, 1981: 189) and the merchant navy were ever badly hit by the manpower demands of war. As far as the latter was concerned, however, there were times, such as during the Seven Years' War, when the general strength of an expanding maritime labour market allowed for the eventual restoration of peacetime manning levels in the merchant fleet during years of war (Starkey, 1990b). On the whole, it appears that the productive capacity of other sectors of the economy was not seriously weakened by the loss of skilled or unskilled workers (O'Brien, 1989a: 336–8; Deane, 1975).

The transfer of able-bodied men from the civilian to the military sector was achieved without recourse to the full-scale conscription of the type introduced by France during the 1790s, even though plans for a British style *levée en masse* were prepared but never implemented by Addington's government in 1803. To some extent this was because there was always, contrary to popular myth, a steady stream of volunteers willing to enter the armed forces. The army made widespread use of regimental recruiting parties which, to the accompaniment of beating drums, scoured the countryside (including Scotland in 1756 and during the 1770s) in search of volunteers. It was only at times of acute manpower shortages that the army had to fall back on the impressment of the unemployed. Such impressment into the army was used during the War of Spanish Succession, when nine recruiting Acts were passed in a twelve-year period, and then again in 1745–6, 1757–8 and 1778–9 (Scouller, 1966: 102–17; Houlding, 1981: 117–19). Both the army and the navy offered incentives in the form of bounties or levy money to would-be soldiers or seamen and, as far as the navy was concerned, this helped to ensure that the recruitment of volunteers represented the main method of solving manning problems. Thus, for example, over 20,000 men came forward for naval service between 1755 and 1757, although the supply dried up for the rest of the Seven Years' War. The navy, which, unlike the army, never took on criminals other than debtors or smugglers, pressed large numbers of merchant seamen into service, and during the mid-1790s two quota Acts extended these powers to include the pressing of 'landsmen'. During every war, naval press gangs operated on land and water in their search for trained seamen, and they were able to achieve considerable success as they patrolled the sea approaches to Britain (Gradish, 1980: 56–86; Baugh, 1965: 157–240; Lloyd, 1968: 124–59; Rodger, 1986: 145–204).

Although great hostility, manifesting itself in violence and disorder, was often directed by the public at large towards the recruiting agencies, the British state was able to make the gradual and potentially difficult transition to the age of mass armed forces without having systematically to coerce a reluctant male civilian population into military service. Impressment played an important part, but patriotic appeals and the prospect of glory and financial reward also helped to ensure that significant numbers of volunteers came forward. Through a little luck, as well as some judgement, and despite specific operations sometimes being hampered by manpower shortages, the authorities were able to meet the nation's military needs without causing serious destabilisation within the economy and society at large. As contemporaries recognised, this represented a considerable achievement. By and large, military performance was sustained without the liberty of the individual being compromised, or essential economic activity being seriously weakened.

A steady flow of volunteers and recruits into the armed forces was needed to offset manpower losses incurred through desertion or death from disease, accident or enemy action. As far as casualties are concerned, however, it is not possible to be precise about the price paid for British military success. It has been calculated that between 1793 and 1815 British deaths amounted to almost 210,000 men (144,000 for the army and 64,000 for the navy), which, in proportionate terms, is greater than those sustained during the First World War (Greenwood, 1942; Emsley, 1979: 169). At times during the wars against Revolutionary and Napoleonic France, deaths fluctuated between 16,000 and 24,000 men a year (Gates, 1994: 137). No general estimates have been made for the other wars of the period, however, and thus it is not possible to compare these losses with those sustained during the earlier years of the eighteenth century. In general, though, in spite of advances made in weaponry and firepower, soldiers and especially sailors had as much to fear from disease and sickness as from enemy action. When, for example, the army left 16,000 men to garrison

Walcheren at the end of the expedition of 1809, malaria struck with such force that within a few months only 4,500 were still fit for duty (Greenwood, 1942). Those serving beyond Europe always ran a strong risk of succumbing to illness, and at times this could devastate British land forces. This was most notably the case in 1741 when the British and American troops assembled to attack Cartegena on the shore of the Caribbean suffered appalling losses from disease and sickness (Harding, 1991).

Losses incurred by the navy through illness represented a serious problem throughout the period, in spite of improvements made to shipboard diet and medicine during the second half of the eighteenth century. This was reflected in the distribution of naval loss between different causes of death. During the Seven Years' War, for example, the navy recorded that only 1,512 men were killed in action, while over 133,000 men were placed under the heading of death (due to disease and accident), desertion or discharge (Rodger, 1986: 147). Between 1776 and 1780, the navy lost 1,243 men in action, but over 18,000 succumbed to disease or illness of one type or another (Duffy 1980: 72; Black, 1994b: 38–9), and it has been estimated that, between 1793 and 1815, 7,000 men were lost to enemy action, 12,000 to shipwreck, and 45,000 to disease (Greenwood, 1942).

If it is not possible to establish overall British manpower losses during the wars of the eighteenth century, there are much firmer statistical grounds when it comes to assessing the financial cost of war to Britain. Above all else, it is abundantly clear that the development of a double-edged military strategy involving a commitment in Europe and the wider world imposed an enormous strain on the nation's financial resources. In part, of course, this was because substantial wartime costs were associated with the recruiting, equipping, provisioning and payment of an ever-increasing number of British troops and sailors. For example, average annual wartime expenditure on the navy alone escalated from £1.8 million during the Nine Years' War to £15.2 million between 1793 and 1815 (Baugh, 1995: 121). In addition, over the period as a whole, considerable sums of money were paid out in the form of subsidies to foreigners who fought on Britain's behalf. At first, these amounts were not enormous by later standards. Between 1701 and 1711, for example, England and Holland pledged to provide around £8 million for their coalition partners, and, in the event, the share paid out by England represented approximately two-thirds of this sum (Dickson and Sperling, 1971: 285). Over time, however, the burden of these payments increased, and between 1702 and 1763 over £24.5 million was spent on foreign troops alone (Brewer, 1989: 32). Even so, this figure pales into insignificance when compared with the subsidies paid by Britain to her allies during the Napoleonic Wars. Sums, which never rose above £2.6 million a year between 1793 and 1807, increased to over £7.5 million a year between 1813 and 1815, with over £20 million being spent on aid and subsidies during the final ten-month campaign of the war (Sherwig, 1969: 354).

Increasing levels of payment to allies were reflected in general expenditure patterns which saw governments spending more money and incurring considerably higher levels of debt during each successive war. Annual public expenditure during wartime rose nearly fourfold from an average of £5,456,555 between 1689 and 1697 to £20,272,700 between 1775 and 1784, and, not surprisingly, the military sector absorbed by far the biggest share of these outgoings. It has been calculated that current military spending (that is expenditure excluding the costs of servicing debts incurred during previous wars) on the army and navy varied between 61 and 74 per cent of total government expenditure during the major wars between 1688 and 1783. This meant that military expenditure represented somewhere between 9 and 14 per cent of national income during that period (Brewer, 1989: 30–41). As many contemporaries observed throughout the long eighteenth century, the outcome of wars was no longer settled by the martial skill and courage of soldiers and seamen alone. It was also dependent upon the ability of states to raise large amounts of money on a regular basis to finance armies and fleets during lengthy conflicts. In the words used by Benjamin Newton in a sermon of 1758, 'the fate of nations' was no longer 'determined by personal Valour and Strength'. Instead, 'The event of war is now generally decided by Profusion of Treasure; the richest Nation is victorious, and the Glorious Wreath of Triumph is become the Price of Gold' (Miller, 1994: 153–4).

The pressure imposed on government finances by these increases in military expenditure was reflected in the substantial growth in the size of unredeemed public debt that was evident at the end of each war. This rose from £16.7 million at the close of the Nine Years' War, through £76.1 million by the conclusion of the War of Austrian Succession, to £242.9 million at the end of the American War of Independence (Brewer, 1989: 30). These amounts, which were always regarded with the utmost alarm by contemporaries, were then thoroughly eclipsed by those generated by the expenditure and debt incurred during the twenty-two year struggle against Revolutionary and Napoleonic France. Annual average gross government expenditure amounted to £79.6 million a year between 1803 and 1815, with peaks of £100 million recorded in each of the climactic years of 1814 and 1815. During these years, military spending averaged £46.2 million a year (37 per cent of which went to the navy), and this accounted for 58.1 per cent of total government expenditure and for approximately 16 per cent of national income. By the end of 1815, the national debt stood at £744.9 million (Mitchell and Deane, 1962: 396, 401–2).

Britain's ever-increasing commitment of human and financial resources to military activity reflected the important changes that occurred in the conduct of warfare during the course of the eighteenth century. War was increasingly expensive, and the army and navy required large numbers of men to undertake active service at home, in Europe, and in the wider world. The mobilisation and effective deployment of these necessary resources posed considerable financial and logistical problems for the state, and the ways in which ministers and officials responded to these problems often served to impose an enormous strain upon the economy and society. At all times, therefore, a fine balance had to be struck between the effective management of the war effort and the need to ensure that government policy did not create economic and social conditions that would provoke threatening levels of internal protest and resistance from a hard-pressed civilian population. How the state attempted to come to terms with this most fundamental of wartime problems is the subject of the next chapter.

3

Taking the strain: state and society

Sustained warfare imposed considerable economic and social strain upon Britain between 1688 and 1815, and the far-reaching nature of government responses to a wide range of war-related pressures and problems defined many of the general features of the newly emerging British state. Indeed, one historian has recently argued that eighteenth-century Britain exhibited all the major characteristics of a 'fiscal-military' state (Brewer, 1989). John Brewer's formulation suggests that, from the Nine Years' War, the implementation of a wide range of war-driven policies had a profound and lasting effect upon the business of government and the activities of the state. This was perhaps most evident in the realm of finance and administration where the introduction of wartime measures was accompanied by necessary improvements and modifications to central government. As a result, an administrative machinery was established which was reasonably efficient by contemporary standards, not least because it was serviced by a growing range of specialist offices and departments staffed by an expanding number of professional public servants. The effects of increased levels of state activity upon the nation at large were felt in a variety of different ways as new taxes were gathered, troops were recruited, and rudimentary social policies were implemented, so that gradually relationships between central government, the state, and the individual were recast. As a result, by 1815 the state intruded into the lives of the civilian population to a much greater degree than had been the case in 1688. Judged in this light, the development of the 'fiscal-military state' represented much more than a means by which Britain was able to meet the challenge of war. Its establishment also acted as an important catalyst for change within society at large.

The funding of war

The severe financial pressures imposed upon the state by the Nine Years' War prompted the development of a whole host of new fund-raising schemes. Many were little more than short-term expedient measures, but others, drawing on a wide range of financial innovations first developed in Europe, had a lasting effect upon the methods used to facilitate tax-gathering, government borrowing, and the transfer of funds. The combined effect was, over time, to transform public finance to such a degree that historians have argued that a 'financial revolution' occurred between 1688 and 1756 (Dickson, 1967). Not only did ministers seek to increase the government's income in time-honoured fashion by raising excise and customs duties, but they introduced new direct taxes, most notably the 'Aid' of 1692, which became the Land Tax. In addition, they also sought to raise funds through the floating of long- and short-term loans. The Tontine loan of 1693, the first of the long-term public loans, was followed by a series of similar annuity loans, and these were supplemented by the funds raised by lottery schemes, the most famous being the Million lottery loan of 1694. Loans were also forthcoming from the great chartered companies. The Bank of England, whose establishment epitomised the innovatory measures of the period, advanced £1.2 million at 8 per cent interest to the state when it was founded in 1694, and the 'new' East India Company offered £2 million at a similar rate four years later. Short-term credit was secured through the issuing of interest bearing bonds by the Exchequer and by the Victualling Office and Navy Board, both of which were heavy-spending government departments requiring ready access to funds. The 1690s were punctuated by acute financial crisis, failure, and uncertainty, and many observers were suspicious about the use of European methods or 'Dutch finance'; but by 1713 Britain had developed reasonably efficient, and above all trusted, methods of fund raising. These were much envied by allies and enemies alike and, over time, they became established on a permanent basis in peace as well as wartime (Dickson, 1967; Dickson and Sperling, 1971; Jones, 1989: 66–94; Neal, 1990: 11–16).

The scale and nature of international conflicts that followed the Nine Years' War made it imperative that ministers maintain reliable and regular channels for raising and deploying the funds and resources necessary to ensure the prosecution of an extended war effort. As already indicated, the sums of money that poured through these channels in wartime were considerable and they greatly increased levels of state spending. Total government expenditure amounted to just over £49 million during the Nine Years' War, but by the Seven Years' War had more than trebled to over £160 million. The length and nature of the French Wars of 1793 to 1815 were reflected in total government expenditure which reached over £1,600 million (Dickson, 1967: 10).

Of course, these figures do not reflect the full extent of government spending on the military, since the financial pressures associated with war did not disappear with the formal cessation of hostilities. Although direct expenditure on the army and navy always fell significantly during every period of peace, the state remained heavily committed to a different, but no less important, form of war-related spending. Government income during wartime was always outstripped to a considerable degree by expenditure, and this ever-increasing shortfall had to be made good through the raising of loans. Indeed, by the time of the War of American Independence, loans were funding almost 40 per cent of government expenditure. Such a dependence upon loan finance meant that returns to peace were always accompanied by the need to continue the payment of substantial amounts of interest on an ever-expanding National Debt. Between 1698 and 1702, peacetime interest payments accounted for 24 per cent of government expenditure, but between 1784 and 1792 they reached a peak of 56 per cent as Pitt the Younger attempted to reduce the burdens imposed by the National Debt (O'Brien, 1988: 2). In broad terms, therefore, expenditure on Britain's armed effort took two forms: current direct spending on the army and navy, and the servicing of earlier war-related debts. It has been calculated that if these two different areas of expenditure are added together they represent, on average, approximately 75 to 85 per cent of annual government spending during the years before 1783 (Brewer, 1989: 40).

The size of the National Debt and its steadily increasing servicing costs offer two clear indications of the degree to which, over time, the state became dependent upon loan finance to fund its military and naval effort. This had been reflected in a marked change in the type of debts incurred by the state during the first quarter of the eighteenth century. In particular, short-term loans, in the form of bills issued by government departments, had been replaced by long-term borrowing arrangements based upon the flotation of government stock or fixed-term redeemable annuities. Accepting the permanent nature of the National Debt, ministers such as Walpole and Pelham moved away from schemes like the Sinking Fund of 1717, designed to reduce the principal of the debt, and instead sought the consolidation and better servicing of that debt, together with the reduction of interest payments (Dickson, 1967: 157–245). The funded debt had replaced the unfunded debt (i.e. those issues not secured on taxes) as the major component of government borrowing by the end of the War of Spanish Succession, and thereafter unfunded debt usually stood at less than 10 per cent of the government's overall commitments (Brewer, 1989: 119–21). The broad restructuring of the way in which the government managed its borrowing requirement had many important consequences, not least of which was a significant rise in the number of public creditors (Dickson, 1967: 285). The development of this large investing community was facilitated by the refinement of mechanisms for the raising of large government loans and by the emergence of a market in transferable securities.

If government borrowing and the development of a well-ordered system of public credit have long been recognised as having been of central importance in the funding of the eighteenth-century state (Dickson, 1967), historians have recently been inclined to place much more emphasis on the part played by the raising of taxes (Brewer, 1989: 88–9). Indeed, O'Brien has gone as far as to suggest that 'The capacity of the English government to levy taxes underpinned and was the prerequisite for Britain's "funding system"'(O'Brien, 1988: 4). This claim is not made because large amounts of tax revenue were diverted into the additional expenditure dedicated to the nation's military and naval effort. Indeed, between 1702 and 1783 about 75 per cent of the extra funds needed to wage war was raised through borrowing. It was only during the French Revolutionary and Napoleonic wars that a fundamental change in the government's approach to war finance resulted in the state managing to generate 58 per cent of its additional financial requirements from tax revenue (Mathias and O'Brien, 1976: 623; O'Brien, 1988: 4). Rather, the general importance of taxation lies in the way that the efficient raising of tax revenue was used to reinforce the system of public credit. Tax revenue ensured that government had a secure and regular flow of income which it could use to maintain its credit and meet its interest payment obligations on specific debts. New debts were underwritten by tax revenues, with the issue of government stock being linked to excises and duties (Dickson, 1967: 71–2; Brewer, 1989: 119). Parliament offered an implicit guarantee that tax revenue would always be collected, and investors were thus able to commit their funds to government loans safe in the knowledge that they would secure a guaranteed risk-free return on their money. Moreover, because they were able to trade their stock in a relatively stable financial market, public creditors were also offered the reassurance of being able to liquidate their assets whenever necessary.

With taxation standing alongside, and interacting with, the system of public credit at the heart of government finance, it was essential that the state was able to expand its tax-raising capacity over time in order to meet the demands imposed by the ever-increasing levels of borrowing. The available evidence suggests that, despite some notable examples of administrative incompetence and low yields, the state was indeed able to secure substantially increased levels of return from taxation during the course of the eighteenth century. Annual tax receipts at the Exchequer rose more than fivefold, from £2.05 million in 1690 to £11.75 million in 1780, whereas new taxation measures introduced during the French wars after 1793 helped to ensure that receipts were increased to £62.67 million by 1815. From these returns, it can be calculated that the share of national income appropriated as taxation grew steadily over time, from 6.7 per cent during the early 1690s, to 11.7 per cent in 1778–82, and to 18.2 per cent in 1812–15 (O'Brien, 1988: 3). This growth in government revenue was considerably greater than that enjoyed by other European states. Early in the period – between 1697 and 1714 – the government in England managed to treble its revenue, while in Holland

and parts of Habsburg empire revenue increased by only a half. In France, where circumstances were very different, government revenue actually fell (Dickson and Sperling, 1971: 313). By the 1780s, rates of per capita taxation in England were two and a half times those in France, and they rose to three times as much during the Napoleonic war (Mathias and O'Brien, 1976). Contrary to popular myth, Britons were not more lightly taxed than their continental counterparts during the eighteenth century. As a recent study of the long-term development of English taxation has emphasised, the fiscal base of the state 'developed haphazardly before the Glorious Revolution but very rapidly thereafter' (O'Brien and Hunt, 1993: 130).

By any standard, these were impressive tax-raising achievements and eighteenth-century European observers regarded Britain with envy, not least because increases in revenue income were secured without serious unrest or civil disturbance. In attempting to explain this British success in the realm of fiscal policy, historians no longer consider increased tax returns to have been a by-product of improved rates of economic growth, not least because in recent years estimates of growth rates have been revised downwards. Instead, attention has been focused on the incidence of taxation and administration of the tax collection system. Although specific measures adopted by ministers during the period enabled government to increase its revenue from taxation, the broad thrust of policy helps to explain why an ever-heavier burden was, for the most part, accepted throughout the nation at large.

Recent work on the British taxation system has emphasised that, although outwardly it shared characteristics with systems elsewhere in Europe, it was nevertheless different in several significant ways. Most importantly, following the ending of tax farming (the system by which the Crown sold the right to collect taxes) during the 1670s and 1680s, the state had assumed a much greater degree of direct responsibility for the collection of revenue. This ensured that many long-standing anomalies, inefficiencies and weaknesses were removed from the system by the beginning of the eighteenth century. The revenue system became open, accountable, subject to regular parliamentary scrutiny, and there were no legal exemptions from individual payment. This helps partly to explain why Britain did not experience serious tax riots during the period. Indeed, it has been pointed out that the major assessed tax, the Land Tax, was widely 'acceptable and accepted'. Although disputes related to the application of county quotas did sometimes cause serious conflicts which surfaced during the General Meetings that were part of the assessment process, it has been argued that 'the administration of the Land Tax was, for the great part of the time, routine and pedestrian' (Brooks, 1974: 282). More often than not, collection procedures were based upon compromise, consent and co-operation. As far as indirect taxes were concerned, historians have perhaps tended to overstate the general efficiency of the customs and revenue system, but collection was effected by an increasing number of professional administrators, and the whole operation was reasonably well ordered, having been centred upon a single controlling body, the Treasury (Binney, 1958: 126–33; Brewer, 1989: 91–114).

At the same time, however, for practical reasons and as part of a considered strategy, the effective tax base proved to be quite narrow, with around 40 per cent of potential revenue not being collected. In part, this was a consequence of deliberate evasion of one sort or another, but it was also because standardised forms of assessment and collection procedure simply could not be implemented effectively by the state across all parts of the country (O'Brien, 1988: 5–6). In many areas, especially those which were remote, local traditions and systems remained in place (Langford, 1991: 161–2), and as a result central government often had to tolerate under assessment of the assessed taxes (Brooks, 1974). Moreover, for much of the period, but especially from Walpole's time, concern was expressed about the need for the expenditure of the poor to be as free as possible from indirect taxation. Exhibiting some degree of social awareness, governments did not impose indiscriminate excise burdens upon goods destined for domestic consumption, and some of the basic items finding their way into the homes of the poor were either lightly taxed or not taxed at all (O'Brien, 1988: 6–13; Langford, 1989: 644–5). This, however, should not be taken to mean that governments failed to exploit domestic consumption as a source for tax revenue. The raising of existing duties was always a favoured option for hard-pressed ministers, and over time more and more items were added to the number of commodities upon which excises were levied. As a result, during the course of this period there were important shifts in the shares of the three major elements – excise, customs and the Land Tax – comprising the government's tax revenues.

Most important of all, after 1714 there was a steady shift from direct to indirect forms of taxation, as the share of total government revenue derived from excise and stamp duties rose sharply from 30 to 57 per cent between 1690 and 1770. Over the same period, the share of customs duties on retained imports moved rather erratically between 20 and 28 per cent. By the late 1790s, each of the two elements within the indirect taxation sector was contributing 36 per cent of total revenue income (O'Brien, 1988: 9–10). The notion that this produced, in general terms, a system that might be defined as 'regressive' – one in which the burden of payment fell in a disproportionately heavy way upon low income groups because of taxes imposed upon essential household goods – has been questioned in recent years. As has been recently pointed out by O'Brien, the authorities sought repeatedly and quite deliberately, to steer away from heavy impositions on 'necessities' such as beer, candles, coal, and soap, and if taxes were imposed upon goods in this category they were usually light and regarded as an exception to the general rule. This attitude became most clearly defined towards the end of the period – during the wars against France – when wealth and luxuries such as coffee, tea, silk and wine bore the heaviest burden of taxation, ensuring that, in theory at least, each section of society contributed to the war effort to a reasonably fair and proportionate degree. Indeed, it has been calculated that over 60 per cent of the extra taxation raised during the French Wars was raised from the 'incomes, and spending patterns of the rich' (O'Brien, 1988: 13).

The steady, deliberate move away from dependence on direct taxation that occurred during the first half of the eighteenth century had been motivated in large part by a political desire, most clearly expressed in Walpole's policies of the late 1720s and early 1730s, to relieve the heavy financial burden placed upon landowners. During the Nine Years' War, almost half of government revenue had been provided by direct taxes, the bulk of which fell exclusively upon members of the aristocracy and landed property owners. In particular, these classes had been affected by statutory arrangements which had obliged them to contribute four shillings in the pound to the 'Aid' of 1692. This measure, an extension of earlier levies, then took on the form of an annual tax on land rents and personal income which by 1698 had become known as the Land Tax. By 1770, the Land Tax continued to be levied at a rate of four shillings in the pound during times of war and at three shillings during times of peace (before the mid 1750s the peace-time rate had stood at two shillings), but the overall tax burden on landowners was lower and direct taxation contributed only 18 per cent of government revenue (O'Brien, 1988: 9–10; Brewer, 1989: 95–9). In part, this was because Land Tax assessment rates had not been altered in line with changes in the real value of land but after 1714 it was also felt that indirect taxation offered a more effective and politically acceptable way forward. Events during the 1690s had demonstrated how difficult it was to collect any form of income tax and ministers had been reluctant to implement the measures necessary to facilitate the accurate assessment of wealth and property. As a result, later administrations were not moved to disturb Land Tax arrangements which provided for local revenue administration and produced a reasonable and elastic yield. Instead, they preferred to rely upon excise duties, taxes on home-produced commodities. Although the excise was extremely unpop-ular, and attempts to extend it to a wider range of goods caused a major political crisis in 1733, it was more easily collected than any direct tax. Because of this, it became the 'major prop of govern-ment finance' (Beckett, 1985: 306).

These general assumptions about government taxation policy were not questioned by those in office until the very end of the eighteenth century. It was only during the late 1790s that funda-mental changes occurred as Pitt the Younger made a concerted effort to secure greater levels of return from direct taxes. This reassessment was prompted by the emergency conditions created by the war against Revolutionary France, which fuelled fears about a rapidly expanding national debt, high interest rates, and the gen-eral state of government credit. Pitt's response to this gathering financial crisis saw the introduction of the short-lived 'triple assess-ment' in 1798, replaced the following year by an income tax which saw the imposition of a graduated levy upon incomes over £60 a year (Cooper, 1982; O'Brien, 1988: 20–2). Even then, however, government revenues continued to be dominated by indirect taxes;

that is by customs duties on imported goods, stamp duties on newspapers and legal documents, and, especially, by excise duties levied upon domestic services and products. The government recognised, like its predecessors, that it could not run the risk of attempting to sustain warfare largely from the proceeds of direct taxation. The state's reliance upon indirect taxes made good administrative, economic and, above all, political sense. If ministers ever doubted that they were set on the most appropriate fiscal course, in terms of both measures and methods, even the most cursory of glances at events in Europe would have reminded them how successful they had been in avoiding serious tax-related revolts and disturbances during the course of the eighteenth century.

Institutional changes: administration and finance

The developments in government funding outlined above prompted the modernisation of the state's administration, and they also led to dramatic changes in the world of high finance. As such, warfare prompted widespread administrative, bureaucratic, and institutional improvements, the deep-felt repercussions of which were felt inside government and, more broadly, within the City of London. As far as government itself was concerned, the formidable task of harnessing and deploying human and financial resources on a vast scale required a considerable administrative effort. The responses to this task saw the gradual development and refinement of a state bureaucracy and infrastructure that was able to sustain, co-ordinate, and regulate a military machine which was seldom inactive for very long. The arrangements put in place during the Nine Years' War were built upon during the War of Spanish Succession when 'an administrative war machinery was established' (Hattendorf, 1978: 24–40). This was a manifestation of the way in which, as one authority has remarked, war acted as the 'great catalyst of [both] administrative discontent and innovation' between 1702 and 1763 (Aylmer, 1980: 93). In large part, this was because the armed forces required direct support from a wide range of government agencies and departments. This meant that within the navy, for example, specialist offices such as the Navy Board, the Victualling Office, the Treasurer's Office and the Sick and Wounded Board took responsibility for different administrative processes associated with recruitment, deployment, supply and welfare, with the whole operation being co-ordinated and super-vised by the Board of Admiralty (Baugh, 1965). The raising of rev-enue was also heavily dependent upon administrative action and procedures, and here an ever-increasing volume of business prompted considerable growth in the total number of government officials. In the realm of fiscal administration, there was a more than threefold increase in the number of full-time employees from just over 2,500 in 1690 to over 8,000 by 1783. Most of this rise took place within the Excise department, which by the 1780s had almost 5,000 employees, thus making it by far the largest of all government departments. Beyond the revenue offices, growth was also occurring, albeit on a far lesser scale, and key departments, such as the Board of Trade, increased their clerical staff during the period so that, in total, there were about 15,000 full-time employ-ees in government service by the middle of the eighteenth century (Brewer, 1989: 65–8).

If Britain's civil and military administration was characterised by expansion, it was also marked by the emergence of newly con-stituted boards and offices alongside departments of state whose lineage could be traced back to the medieval royal household. This served to produce, in overall terms, a system containing many anomalies and inconsistencies, and there was plenty of scope for corruption, inefficiency, and incompetence on a grand scale (Aylmer, 1980: 106). Yet, as has recently been pointed out, new methods and procedures, the emergence of the career administra-tor in place of, or alongside, the sinecure holder, an improving atti-tude towards public service, and regular auditing, inquiry and parliamentary review, all combined to create a bureaucratic envi-ronment in which better administration and higher standards of official conduct were cultivated (Brewer, 1989: 69–85).

As far as taxation was concerned, the state assumed more direct responsibility for the collection of revenue and this ensured that procedures became well-ordered, uniform and professionally administered under the close supervision of central government agencies. This was not the case, however, with the Land Tax. Its assessment and collection remained in the hands of commissioners and locally appointed officers and, as noted earlier, the effective-ness of their actions was often patchy, especially in the outlying parts of Britain. On the other hand, it now seems beyond dispute that excise and stamp duties were raised and administered by a government department whose measurement and recording procedures were reasonably efficient and well-ordered (Brewer, 1989: 101–14). The long arm of the Excise office reached into all corners of eighteenth-century England (the picture is far less clear for Scotland and Wales), and its field officers, often the only state official seen in many places, came to represent a 'symbol of a new form of government' (Brewer 1989: 114). This was a form of government in which a few highly centralised 'modern' elements had been grafted on to a system still characterised, in general terms, by the exercise of authority by unpaid local magistrates and sheriffs drawn from the ranks of the gentry (Langford, 1991: 390–410). Indeed, if anything, as far as the routine administration of the realm was concerned, more responsibility was transferred to the localities which were not, as in other European countries, being subjected to increased levels of control from the centre (Innes, 1994: 118). In overall terms, this proved to be a form of government whose long-term effectiveness was based upon an ability to adapt to wartime conditions in ways which revealed it to be 'in structural terms flexible and resilient rather than aggressive or authoritarian' (Langford, 1989: 693).

The raising of large amounts of loan finance was not a task that could be undertaken by the state in the same way as the collection and administration of taxes. Out of necessity, ministers had to draw upon the skills and resources of intermediary financiers and agencies and, in this context, the establishment of the Bank of England in 1694 was of the greatest importance. The Bank's primary function was to act as a 'money-raising machine', and in the short term it performed this task by drawing £1.2 million from subscribers, a sum upon which the interest payments to stockholders were secured by specific taxes. The general circumstances of the eighteenth century, with war following war, dictated that, although the arrangements of 1694 might have been regarded as a temporary measure born out of crisis, by the 1720s the Bank occupied a position of central importance in the funding of the state. Ministers turned to it again and again during times of need (Bowen, 1995: 3–6). Although its early years were far from untroubled, most notably during the aftermath of the great recoinage of

1696, the Bank's developing strengths and resources became such that ministers came to regard it as the linchpin of the state's funding system. By 1749, the Bank had advanced over £11.5 million to the state. Because of this, and in spite of experimentation with alternative schemes (such as the unsuccessful flotation of a rival Land Bank in 1696), governments were always prepared to renew and extend the Bank's monopolistic privileges and terms of reference. The Bank's charter was renewed six times between 1696 and 1781, reflecting that the Bank had become, in the words of Adam Smith, the 'great engine of state' (Bowen, 1995: 2). It improved public borrowing, handled the administration of the national debt, serviced the financial needs of the army and navy, and engaged in the routine management of many areas of government departmental finance. By the end of the eighteenth century, the overall effect of these war-related developments had brought about 'an administrative shift from the Exchequer to the Bank' (Binney, 1958: 92), a change which symbolised the broad restructuring that had taken place within the conduct and management of government business since 1688.

The forging of a close relationship of mutual benefit between the state and the Bank of England also had significant effects within the wider economy. The arrangements put in place during the 1690s facilitated the emergence of the Bank as a reliable bank of issue for London and the Home Counties, a function that had been uppermost in the minds of many of those who had promoted the idea of a bank in the first place. Secured firmly upon government revenue, the Bank was able to offer credit facilities, develop its own private business, and, as it increased its reserves, it supported notes in circulation. The Bank was well regarded by London's merchant and business community, and it came to be regarded as a fundamentally sound institution. By the mid-eighteenth century, its strength and reputation was such that it was adopting the role of lender of last resort during times of financial crisis, and through the discretionary use of discounting it was able to 'apply a restraining hand in the economy' (Lovell, 1957: 17). Emerging from, and dependent upon, the Bank's role as 'banker to the state' were no less important functions related to circulation and credit within the economy at large.

The wartime conditions that led to the establishment of the Bank of England also provided the broad context for the emergence in London of a market in transferable stocks and shares. This market was built upon existing banking, credit, and insurance facilities located in and around Exchange Alley, and practices and procedures were refined by financial experts, many of whom had moved to England from Europe during the turbulent years at the end of the seventeenth century (Neal, 1990: 11–18). As a result, an increasingly specialised financial service sector developed to cater for those who wished to invest in stock, shares and government loans. The brokers, 'jobbers', and bankers who operated in this sector, together with the large-scale investors who provided funds for the government, were indiscriminately labelled as the 'monied interest'. They often received hostile criticism from those who were deeply suspicious about the way in which this new and ever-changing world of high finance was developing. Whereas it could be argued that financial innovation was essential for sustaining successive war efforts, the side effects, especially the development of speculative activity, were often thought to be disturbing the nation's socio-economic structure and undermining its moral strength (Dickson, 1967: 486–520; Bowen, 1993).

The nascent stock market offered a wide range of investing options, from short-term investment in government bills of various kinds to longer-term commitment to annuities, stock or the shares of the 'monied' chartered companies. Their availability attracted a diverse range of individuals who all contributed to the creation of an investing culture, the strength of which was reflected in the rapid growth that occurred in the number of public creditors. As the size of the National Debt increased remorselessly after mid-century, the number of public creditors expanded from 60,000 or so during the 1750s to about half a million by 1815. Most of these investors were drawn from London and the south of England, but there was also sizeable, if diminishing, number from Europe, notably the United Provinces (Dickson, 1967: 249–337). The deployment of their financial resources into different forms of state activity was essential for enabling Britain to come to terms with the strains imposed by more than a century of international conflict and warfare.

Social problems and the response of the state

Within society at large, economic and social problems caused, or exacerbated, by war fuelled a simmering discontent which at times of acute tension was often translated into civilian disorder and unrest. This was especially the case during the difficult years at the end of the eighteenth century when the ideological and political consequences of the French Revolution were being felt across Europe. Between 1793 and 1801, there were several mutinies in different branches of the armed forces (including the famous Spithead and Nore naval mutinies of 1797 and 1798), as well as violent clashes between civilians and either military units or officials who supervised the collection of the excise or Land Tax. There was also widespread discontent caused by recruitment into the army, navy and militia (see below: 51–52). At the same time, a different type of social tension was fuelled by the hardships caused by rising prices and grain shortages, and serious disturbances occurred, notably in southern England in 1795, when disaffected troops or militiamen acted in concert with the local population in order to secure food supplies and fix prices. There were further food-related disturbances at times of harvest failure in 1800–1 and 1810–13, and after 1810 there was also a wave of machine-breaking riots in northern industrial towns as skilled artisans gave vent to their disaffection and frustration with new working conditions and practices (Jones, 1973; Stevenson, 1974; Boshedt, 1983; Wells, 1986; Wells, 1988: 99–106). All in all, a wide range of grievances, national and local, economic, political and social, combined to create deeply unsettled wartime conditions across many parts of England and Wales (Boshedt, 1983: 14–26).

More generally, war-related social tensions were created throughout the eighteenth century when large numbers of men were taken up by the armed forces during times of conflict only to be released back into civilian society at the cessation of hostilities. Regular expansions and contractions of the army had an extremely disruptive and dislocating effect upon family and community life, even though in the short term the outbreak of war helped in some ways to ease some of the worst tensions within society. This occurred when unemployed workers and 'undesirables' were transferred from the civilian sector into military service, the movement of adult males providing welcome relief in an economy and society in which there was a very large pool of casual and temporary labourers, as well as those who were 'idle' or destitute. Not surprisingly, however, the return of peace was always widely feared because these unfortunates were unceremoniously cast back into communities that offered them little by way of effective support or employment opportunities. Official desire to see drastic reductions in the size of the armed forces during the first years of all periods of peace prompted the large-scale demobilisation of members of the army and navy. A Royal Naval establishment of 76,000 in 1763 was, for example, cut to only 17,500 within a year (Duffy, 1980: 56), but at least some of those released by the navy held the prospect of finding employment in a merchant fleet long starved of officers and men. Those in the army were not so fortunate, and the effects of the return of large numbers of demobilised men into society could be considerable. It has been estimated that the number of men leaving the services totalled around 157,000 in 1713–14 and 160,000 in 1784–5, and perhaps over 300,000 men flooded back into society in 1815 at the end of the Napoleonic War (Hay, 1982: 139; Beattie, 1986: 226). Not only did this represent somewhere between 1 and 3 per cent of the entire population, but also it included a very significant proportion of the most vulnerable adult male labouring classes.

A repeated inability to absorb former soldiers and sailors successfully back into the community has prompted one historian to describe demobilisation as a 'disaster', the legacy of which constituted a 'constant peacetime problem' throughout the eighteenth century (Hay, 1982: 141). At a time when war-related industries were contracting, the outlook and prospects for many demobilised men were very bleak indeed, and their position worsened further when their return into society coincided with food shortages, as in 1783. Vagrancy became a serious problem, and many discharged men often resorted to crime, a course of desperate action clearly reflected in statistics which indicate sharp increases in the number of indictments for theft during the first years of every period of peace. Although firm evidence is only available for one or two areas, notably parts of Surrey and Staffordshire, it nevertheless suggests that movements between war and peace bore directly upon marked fluctuations – a series of peaks and troughs – in levels of property-related crime. The highest levels of prosecution and indictment were experienced (and sustained) during years of peace when 'normal' economic conditions, including widespread unemployment and underemployment, were re-established. On the other hand, levels of crime were significantly reduced during periods of conflict when war-related activities expanded and the armed forces were obliged to call upon the services of the most dangerous and desperate elements within the labouring classes. So clearly evident was this pattern to contemporaries that the return of peace was always accompanied by general expressions of fear about rising levels of crime. To many, such concerns represented a heavy price to be paid for military success in Europe and further afield (Hay, 1982; Beattie, 1986: 213–32).

Although eighteenth-century governments seldom hesitated before introducing repressive legislation, or putting a violent end to riot and insurrection, they also displayed an increasing willingness to relieve the various forms of hardship caused by war. The measures introduced were piecemeal and only ever had a very limited effect upon the serious problems they were designed to address. Nevertheless, they represented an acknowledgement by those in authority that the state had at least a degree of responsibility to offer basic levels of support to the victims of war. This meant that, in addition to the opening of various relief subscription funds, and the establishment of charitable self-help projects, such as the soup kitchens and food-distribution networks that appeared during the acute distress of the 1790s and 1800s (Wells, 1988: 214–15, 224–25, 227; Boshedt, 1982: 91, 95–8), some basic hardship provision was administered by the state or local authorities for the benefit of servicemen, ex-servicemen and their dependants.

During the 1690s, hospitals had been built for former soldiers at Chelsea, and for aged and infirm sailors at Greenwich, the latter institution being funded by a 6d a month deduction from the wages of all merchant and naval seamen. In an attempt to replace the use of unsatisfactory hospital ships and contract hospitals, the navy also opened a large infirmary, the Royal Hospital, at Haslar near Gosport. This institution, which cost £100,000 (and was one of the largest brick buildings in Europe) took its first patients in 1754, and six years later the doors were opened at a hospital built at Stonehouse near Plymouth. Both hospitals set new standards of hygiene and care, and were able to cope with several hundred sick patients at any one time (Gradish, 1980: 172–202; Rodger, 1986: 109–12). The number of 'out pensioners' supported by the Chelsea and Greenwich hospitals grew considerably after 1713 and 1763 respectively. Special relief payments were made to disabled sailors and naval widows from the 'Chatham Chest', which had been established in Elizabethan times and was also funded by contributions from seamen's wages. Furthermore, allowances were paid from poor-relief funds to the dependants of those serving in the militia who were posted away from home during wartime. Some limited efforts were made to ease the way of demobilised servicemen into civilian society, although they appear to have met with little success (Ehrman, 1953: 130–1, 441–4; Innes, 1994: 108–17).

As far as the distressed civilian population were concerned, by the beginning of the nineteenth century there was at least some recognition in central and local government circles that positive action was needed during periods of harvest failure and food shortages. Indeed, these problems could hardly be ignored between 1793 and 1815 when inflationary pressures caused general price increases of around 70 per cent (Flinn, 1974; Gourvish, 1976). As far as basic foodstuffs were concerned, the price of wheat trebled from 43 shillings a quarter in 1792 to 126 shillings a quarter in 1812, and the cost of a 4 lb loaf of bread in London increased from 6d to 1s 5d during the same twenty-year period (Mitchell and Deane, 1962: 488, 498). It was against this general background, in 1795, that the Berkshire magistrates, meeting at Speenhamland, responded to the acute crisis caused by high food prices by introducing the practice of supplementing the low wages of able-bodied workers with poor-relief payments. In fact, the use of scales to determine additional payments for poverty-stricken labourers originated, and had already been applied, elsewhere, but the Speenhamland scale attracted much attention and soon became widely known. Indeed, historians have long referred to the 'Speenhamland system'. The scale was introduced across much of southern England after 1795 and, although the long-term effects of this have been the subject of considerable debate, it provided much-needed assistance for the hard-pressed rural population during wartime (Oxley, 1974: 109–19).

If the introduction of the Speenhamland scale represented an initiative developed by those who had to deal with severe poverty at local level, other responses to the food crisis were formulated at national level. Between 1794 and 1796, and then again between 1799 and 1801, the export of cereals from Britain was prohibited and the duties payable on imported grain were reduced or suspended. Pitt's government began to organise and deal directly in grain supplies from Canada and Northern Europe in 1795, an action which has been described as marking perhaps 'the first example of state trading in essential supplies' (Stern, 1964: 178). This scheme was soon abandoned in favour of arrangements which offered bounty payments to grain-importing merchants (Wells, 1988: 184–95), although throughout the period the government remained resolutely opposed to intervention in the management of the nation's internal grain trade. The implementation of these measures, which provoked intense political debate about the desirability of government involvement in the workings of the market, had the effect of boosting grain imports to a significant degree, but action was also necessary to ensure that levels of consumption were brought more closely in line with supply. Voluntary retrenchment was encouraged, and bans were imposed upon the distillation of wheat and the sale of hot or fresh bread. In addition, a range of initiatives were launched in an attempt to promote grain substitution, the consumption of reduced quality or 'brown' bread, and the more extensive use of meat, rice and vegetables (especially in the form of soup) in working-class diets (Wells, 1988: 184–229). As with other welfare initiatives, some of these actions, particularly those associated with attempts to change diets, were often unpopular and their effects were very limited. They do indicate, however, that in certain circumstances, not least those which promoted fears of widespread disorder, wartime conditions could lead to intervention by the authorities in the workings of the economy and society at large.

The stresses and strains that war imposed upon British society during this period were varied and considerable, and, as a result, many Britons experienced severe hardship, misery and poverty. Yet for all the economic and social tensions that emerged, Britain managed to avoid the serious dangers associated with national bankruptcy and political and social unrest of the type experienced in France during the revolutionary period. The late-eighteenth-century margin of comfort is a matter for vigorous debate among some historians (Christie, 1984; Wells, 1986), but survival in itself represents a considerable (and often overlooked) achievement. The state's internal structures and institutions overcame the test of war, albeit often in modified form, suggesting that the strategic approach to war was complemented by administrative, fiscal and social policies that were reasonably sensitive to the capacity and ability of the British people to sustain successive wartime efforts over a long period of time.

4

A nation in arms: the armed forces and British society

Although Britain was at war for much of the eighteenth century, the nature of the relationship between military activity and British society was defined by circumstances which dictated that very little armed conflict actually took place on home soil. Britons were fortunate that their geographical position helped to protect them from some of the most damaging effects of war. The Jacobite risings of 1715 and 1745, together with a few failed invasion attempts, represented only brief and short-lived experiences of war at first hand. Moreover, Britain did not suffer demographic loss, devastation and destruction on anything like the scale of those European states whose territories provided the arenas where large armies manoeuvred and fought (Anderson, 1989: 136–8).

These circumstances ensured that the wartime experiences of British civilians, especially those in England and Wales, were quite different from many of their continental counterparts who found that the structures and rhythms of their everyday life were repeatedly disrupted by the prosecution and consequences of war. Richard Price, the Dissenting minister and moral philosopher, paid particular attention to this when he preached a sermon on the Day of General Thanksgiving that followed the great victories of 1759, and his comments bear testimony to Britain's general good fortune in war during the eighteenth century. Observing that the nation was secure behind its ocean wall, he declared that 'We live in the quiet and full possession of all our properties and blessings, without being in any danger from the inroads of enemies.' Because of this, he continued, 'We *hear* indeed of the dreadful calamities and desolations of war, but we only *hear* of them. We neither *feel* nor *see* them.' He concluded that there was 'little difference between the state of most of us now, and what it was before the commencement of war', and thus, as far as most citizens were concerned, 'was it not for the accounts we read and the reports conveyed to us, we should scarcely know that we are engaged in war' (Thomas, 1992: 2–3). Price was undoubtedly carried away on a strong-running tide of public celebration and rejoicing when he made these observations, but he was accurate in his assessment that the vast majority of British civilians did not have first-hand experience of military action at close quarters. Nevertheless, his comments should not be taken to mean that war was always remote and bore lightly upon the population at large. Although it is possible to read some civilian wartime diaries and memoirs in which military activity is only dimly or intermittently perceived, it is evident that in some parts of the country, notably southern England, the effects of war were often keenly felt by ordinary people who were not themselves members of the armed forces. They were aware of troops on the move; they witnessed the establishment of large, if temporary, military camps; they participated in the industrial and agricultural effort that was necessary to keep armies in the field and ships on the sea; and perhaps they even saw some of the quarter of a million or so enemy prisoners of war in port towns and elsewhere who were held in Britain at one time or another between 1793 and 1815 (Crimmin, 1996). Their individual experiences, and to an extent their lifestyles, were conditioned by the nation being often braced in a state of readiness against the threat of invasion for long periods of time. Equally, they were affected by circumstances in which the length and frequency of conflict was increasingly reflected in the way that military influences were brought to bear both upon, and within, society at large.

The legacy of war

Although many of the institutional and bureaucratic features of the eighteenth-century British state were shaped by the demands of war, there were formal limits to the extent to which military influence was allowed to pervade and shape society at large. In part, this was because, unlike many continental 'absolutist' rulers, British monarchs and their ministers were not given a free hand to raise and deploy large numbers of troops at home or abroad. The tumultuous dynastic and political events of the mid-seventeenth century had helped to develop a strong anti-militarist tradition which found legislative expression in measures implemented in the wake of the 'Glorious Revolution' of 1688–9. In particular, fears that a despotic monarch might once more use a standing army to threaten hard-won civil liberties were translated into attempts to remove direct control of the military from the king. This ensured that '1688 brought a profound and lasting alteration in the relations between the Crown, Parliament, and the army' (Childs, 1994: 60). The Bill of Rights of 1689 therefore included an important clause to curb royal power which stated that 'the raising or keeping of a standing army within this kingdom in time of peace unless it be with the consent of Parliament is against the law'. In practice, this meant that the annual debate on the Mutiny Bill developed into an occasion after 1713 when Parliament sanctioned the number of troops to be kept on the establishment each year (Chandler, 1994: 93). This, together with the frequency of war and the need to raise and disband troops on a regular basis, helped to keep the issue alive throughout the first half of the eighteenth century, and it fuelled intense debate about the appropriate place for armed forces within British society. The whole question of the relationship between the military and civil branches of society was kept firmly in the public eye and, particularly during the early part of the century, it represented an emotive political issue (Dickinson, 1977: 104–6).

If contemporaries feared that a standing army might be used as a tool of repression and tyranny, historians have been more inclined to consider the ways in which such an army acted to promote military influence within British society. This is an important issue, because not only was Britain at war for much of the century but developments on the continent saw the emergence of several states in which civilian society was organised to a considerable degree along lines dictated by the armed forces. As far as Britain was concerned, it is quite clear that military influence was heavily felt in many areas of civilian life during times of war. However, in determining whether or not the eighteenth-century British state was 'militarised' to anything like the same degree as Prussia or Austria, perhaps the most important test is that which considers the extent to which military influence continued to be felt throughout society during years of peace.

At the cessation of hostilities, Britain was always swift to reduce the size of its armed forces through the large-scale demobilisation of troops and sailors. Not only were there plenty of lingering political fears about the potential threat to liberty posed by standing armies but, more importantly, there was widespread concern about the effects that high levels of peacetime military expenditure would have upon an ever-expanding national debt. The consequences of this instinctive response meant that the pattern of peace and war led to many short-term violent swings in the numbers of men that Britain had under arms at any one time. Rapid demobilisations ensured that the years of peace always saw a military and naval establishment standing at a level that was considerably lower than that maintained during wartime, even though the overall size of peacetime forces increased steadily over time. During the 1730s, for example, the navy was manned by no more than 8,000 sailors, having touched a low point of 6,298 in 1724, but by the mid- and late 1760s its notional peacetime strength had risen to around 16,000 men (Davis, 1962: 321; Lloyd, 1968: 286–9). In spite of this net increase, which helped to ensure that average annual peacetime expenditure on the navy doubled from £1 million between 1715 and 1739 to over £2 million between 1784 and 1792 (Baugh, 1995: 121), the ratio of wartime to peacetime naval manpower remained fairly constant at around five to one.

There was not always such a great difference between wartime and peacetime establishments as far as the army was concerned, even though at times, such as during the great reduction of 1712–13 or in the period after the War of American Independence, it could be reduced rapidly to a state of 'dereliction' (Gates, 1994: 133). In general, as with the growth in the size of the navy, the number of men on the notional peacetime British establishment rose, from 18,000 in the late 1720s to 30,000 by the early 1750s, and the latter level of manning was maintained at the end of the Seven Years' War (Rogers, 1977: 17–31; Guy, 1985: 9–10). Although a rising number of troops from regiments of foot had to be deployed in overseas garrisons (Houlding, 1981: 4–7), the bulk of this force was kept at home during peacetime and the British mainland could be reinforced at short notice by some of the troops based in Ireland, who were kept on a separate establishment and funded by Irish tax revenues. The existence of this Irish establishment, which had been fixed at 12,000 men in 1692 and was increased to 15,300 men in 1769, meant that the overall size of the peacetime British army stood at around 30,000 men for much of the first half of the century, before it rose to 45,000 men during the 1760s (Houlding, 1981: 9–11). In addition, of course, in England and Wales the presence of the armed forces was reinforced by the militia which remained in being in the years of peace after 1763, although in many counties the organisation fell into a state of decay and its members were seldom if ever mustered. All in all, therefore, it seems reasonable to conclude that the size of the land forces maintained during peacetime stood somewhere between a quarter and a half of the total number of troops mobilised by Britain during times of war.

The details outlined above illustrate in simple numerical terms that the military presence in peacetime Britain increased quite considerably as the eighteenth century unfolded. But, of course, they do not by themselves provide firm evidence that society itself was becoming militarised to any great degree. The function and role of the armed forces, together with the general nature of the relationship between the military and civil authorities, require examination because it is these factors which help to define the general social, political and cultural characteristics of any society.

Although just prior to the period under review, low levels of pay had often obliged soldiers to live and work among the civilian population during peacetime, the armed forces did not intrude very far into the everyday lives of many ordinary people during the eighteenth century. In architectural terms, for example, military activity did not leave a very heavy imprint on the land or townscape. This was despite a small boom in military building inspired by Sir John Vanbrugh after 1715, and later notable construction projects such as the Royal Military College and Royal Artillery barracks at Woolwich (1775–1808) and the Royal Military Academy at Sandhurst (1807–12) (Cruickshank, 1985: 155). These were followed by the building of prisons or depots to house large numbers of prisoners of war during the French wars of 1793 to 1815 (Crimmin, 1996). Moreover, even though some areas of strategic importance such as Ireland, Scotland, and especially the south and east coast of England, were reinforced, notably during the Napoleonic war, through

the building of forts, Martello towers, or defensive structures such
the Royal Military Canal in Kent, many of these installations were
often unoccupied, left in a state of disrepair, and located well away
from civilian communities (Longmate, 1991: 274–83; Glover, 1973:
103–24). Unlike many parts of western Europe, where architects
such as Vauban and Coehoorn designed elaborate defensive structures to protect ports and frontier urban centres, Britain, as foreign
visitors often observed, did not possess large numbers of fortified
towns and villages. Even though a major dockyard town such as
Portsmouth was heavily defended by British standards, it failed to
impress some contemporaries. In 1708, one observer described the
town, like all the other dockyard towns, as 'a long time neglected and
gone to ruin', a circumstance which rendered it 'like a gate without
locks, bolts and bars' (Hattendorf, 1987: 176). From a defensive
point of view, things improved in the dockyard towns thereafter
(Coad, 1989), but for the most part urban life and development in
Britain did not take place within contexts defined by military needs
and imperatives. This meant that there were few remaining traces of
the type of 'garrison government' that had existed during some of
the more tumultuous periods of the seventeenth century, when civilian activities had been constrained by the demands imposed upon
the population by local military commanders.

Few permanent barracks were built in England before the
1790s, although a notable exception was provided by those con-
structed at Berwick in 1717. These reflected official concern about
the situation in Scotland, and a number of strategically placed
forts and garrisons were also established north of the border in the
wake of the Jacobite risings of 1715 and 1745. It was only after
1792, however, that a wholehearted commitment was made to barrack building in England, first in response to internal unrest and
then later to the threat from Revolutionary and Napoleonic
France. The latter fear ensured that most of the 168 barracks of all
types established by 1805 were situated in coastal areas and, in
total, these assorted collections of buildings were eventually capable of housing over 130,000 troops (Emsley, 1983).

During the eighteenth century, peacetime garrisons tended to
be very small indeed. Only infantry troops were ever billeted in
towns, with cavalry units being stationed in the countryside near
major centres of population (Childs, 1982: 185–9). For much of its

time, the army was on the move between duty areas and a combination of quartering problems and the nature of peacetime duties meant that units were often broken up and dispersed over wide areas (Houlding, 1981: 23–45). Emergency situations could dictate that the distribution of these troops could become extremely uneven and in 1768, for example, concerns about the Wilkite riots in London led to eight of the thirteen regiments of foot being stationed in the south of England, leaving one in the north, and four in Scotland (Hayter, 1978: 23). This meant that, although attempts were made to ensure 'there was hardly a corner of England and Wales that was not within easy reach of a Company of soldiers' (Childs, 1982: 186), there were often lengthy periods of time when citizens in some areas never set eyes upon any troops at all. This was particularly the case in inaccessible parts of the country such as north Wales, north Devon, and the trans-Pennine region, whereas in Scotland there was never much of a regular army presence other than during the occupations that followed in the wake of uprisings (Houlding, 1981: 25–7). The situation was rather different in other parts of the country, especially around London and across southern England, where guard and coastal duties always occupied large numbers of troops. Of course, it was this area, from Suffolk to Dorset, which also saw greatly increased levels of military activity during wartime as troops were moved to embarkation points, defences were strengthened, and large temporary training camps were established in places such as Salisbury, Coxheath near Maidstone, and Tiptree Heath in Essex.

The low profile maintained by the armed forces in many parts of the country helped to emphasise the clear dividing line between the civil and military branches within British society. This division was increasingly reinforced by the willingness of the army and navy to adopt standardised forms of organisation, discipline and uniform. It not only made them more effective and professional but also enabled them to develop their own sense of distinct identity, separateness, and esprit de corps. Though both the army and the navy evolved into well-defined societies in their own right, at no stage did this process lead to the extension of military authority and power into areas beyond the armed forces. This was because the armed forces existed as elements within a much broader civil society which kept them firmly in a position of subordination and dependency and, for example, the military were never able to exert concerted influence in the offices of state or Parliament (Brewer, 1989: 42–55). Although several aspects of state activity were shaped to a considerable degree by the needs of the armed forces, the strength and formality of the relationship between the civil and military branches of society helped to ensure that the development of British society as a whole was never directed and organised along general lines of the type evident in the militarised and absolutist states of Austria and Prussia (Anderson, 1989: 167–80).

Military influence in British society

If, in a physical sense, the army and navy appeared increasingly to stand apart from the population at large, several strong traces of military influence were nevertheless evident throughout mainstream British society in peacetime and war. At the highest level, the royal family set a general tone by fully acknowledging the part played by the military in both sustaining the regime and enhancing British power. Although Parliament had asserted its control over the armed forces in the wake of the Glorious Revolution, British monarchs sought, like their continental counterparts, to be soldier kings, and this meant that they and their sons took an active part in general leadership and supervision of the armed forces. The prime example was set by the sixty-year old George II who was the last king to lead his troops into battle, at Dettingen in 1743. Three years later, his son William, duke of Cumberland, was the notorious victor over the Jacobite army at Culloden, although his attempts during the Seven Years' War to continue the family military tradition on the battlefield proved to be unsuccessful. And, later, although George III's second son, Frederick Augustus duke of York (captured in popular memory by a nursery rhyme) did not enjoy great success on the battlefield, he served with some distinction as a reforming Commander-in-Chief of the army at a difficult time during the wars against Revolutionary and Napoleonic France (Gates, 1994: 144–5).

In overall terms, the effects of parliamentary restraints, together with the general nature of the military decision-making process and command structure, ensured that British monarchs were unable fully to translate their personal military wishes into action, and the extent of their direct control over the army never approached the levels exerted by Frederick the Great over Prussian forces (Guy, 1985: 19–23). None the less, all monarchs, with the notable exception of Queen Anne, took a keen and detailed interest in military and naval affairs. They paid close attention to senior appointments and promotions, spent a great deal of time reviewing troops and fleets, and were often responsible for initiating a wide range of important reform measures (Guy, 1994: 98–9). George I took the lead in establishing annual inspections, and he regulated the buying and selling of commissions, whereas George II and George III each displayed a keen interest in the development and standardisation of drill and regulations for the army (Houlding, 1981: 100; Gates, 1994: 141; French, 1990: 37). These enthusiasms ensured that there was always a military dimension to life at court, and this was reflected in codes of dress and etiquette which, in turn, found expression in the way that royal portrait artists often depicted their subjects in full army or naval uniform.

Taking a lead from their monarch, the aristocracy focused considerable attention on the army and navy, even if at local level they were often reluctant to present themselves for part-time service in the militia (Langford, 1991: 298–300). Entry to the armed forces offered opportunities to the second and third sons of aristocrats, and service enhanced their prestige and status. Some peers took advantage of political connections and patronage to secure high office at the Admiralty, the Navy Board or the War Office, but many more of the elite began to pursue active service careers in the field or at sea. There was a significant level of noble representation in the navy where a professional and well-regarded officer corps developed during the first half of the eighteenth century, whereas the higher echelons of the army were densely populated with peers and the sons of peers (Rodger, 1986: 252–327; Baugh, 1965: 93–146; Cannon, 1984: 118–23; Duffy, 1980: 62–6; Roy, 1987). This underlined the extent to which serving the state had begun to form a core element within elite lifestyles, and the process had been reinforced in a formal sense after 1714 by the granting of half-pay in peacetime to all army and navy officers who were no longer on active service (Brewer, 1989: 56, 58). The importance of military service was also enhanced by the increasingly pervasive influence of what has been described as an 'ostentatious cult of heroism' (Colley 1992: 178). This cult found expression in a number of different ways, from the artistic depiction of the nation's military and naval heroes such as Nelson, through the representation of military themes on the theatrical stage (Russell, 1995), to the wearing of colourful decorated uniforms. Such was the widespread sartorial effect of the latter development that it has been held to have represented a 'revolution in the appearance of the British male elite' (Colley, 1992: 177–93). Thus, if Britain did not possess a *noblesse d'épée* of the formal type evident in pre-Revolutionary France, it is nevertheless clear that powerful elite influence was brought to bear upon, and within, the armed forces, and the strength of the aristocratic connection helped to define the ways in which military mores and values were extended into society at large. Indeed, the symbiotic nature of the relationship between the army and the genteel classes ensured that in some parts of the wider world the officer corps became a powerful agency for the diffusion of metropolitan aristocratic and gentlemanly ideals into colonial societies (Shy, 1965).

As far as ordinary citizens were concerned, apart from service in the armed forces or militia, peacetime contact with the army could take a number of different forms. In England and Wales, small groups of troops were, in the absence of adequate barrack facilities, billeted in public and private houses; in Scotland, soldiers were used to gather taxes and, under the supervision of General Wade, built roads during the 1720s (Anderson 1989: 185–6, 197; Houlding, 1981: 34–5). A significant number of civilian workers played some part in the various processes that fed into the systems of military production, provisioning and supply. Above all, however, troops became most conspicuous when, in the absence of a proper police force, they were asked to preserve law and order. They performed a variety of tasks. They were used by the Secretary at War, who held ultimate responsibility for such matters, to bring riots and disorder under control, and they carried out a range of anti-smuggling, escort, guard, and police duties in support of local authorities and the agents of central government such as excise officers (Hayter, 1978; Houlding, 1981: 57–74). At times, some of these tasks could be dangerous and onerous, none more so when events, such as the Wilkite Riots of 1768 or the Gordon Riots of 1780, led to a near-complete breakdown of law and order in parts of London. But although the state was often dependent upon the army to help it overcome social and political unrest, military force never threatened to become an uncontrolled or unregulated power in the land. Fears about despotism and threats to individual liberty ensured that in England and Wales, if not Ireland and Scotland, the power of the army was always held firmly in check, and there were many legal restrictions prohibiting or regulating the use of military force against the civilian population (Hayter, 1978: 9–19). As a result, local army commanders found their authority subordinated to that of the civil authorities and this meant that they were never able to act on their own initiative in response to riot and disorder. More generally, members of the armed forces could not behave towards the public in an arbitrary fashion as if they had been freed from the constraints imposed by civil law. Except in a few very rare emergency situations, all military codes of behaviour and discipline were overridden by the law of the land, and this ensured that the population were offered a full degree of protection from the armed forces (Brewer, 1989: 47–9).

Over time, a number of factors contributed to a reduction in public fears about the army and the unregulated use of military force within society at large. Serious disturbances continued to raise questions about civil–military relations, but by the middle of the eighteenth century the standing army no longer represented a central element within the broad range of issues which provided the staple diet for political discourse. In part, this was because events had demonstrated that, although the army had an important role to play in civil society, it had been brought under the firm control of Parliament since 1688. Its actions were thus regulated by the constraints imposed by civil law as well as by its own internal codes of discipline. As such, by the second half of the eighteenth century, 'militarism', or the deployment of force by a foreign-born absolute or despotic monarch, was no longer seen to represent a threat to liberty (Langford, 1989: 687–9). There was also a marked transformation in public attitudes towards the army during the Seven Years' War (Guy, 1994: 110). Britons were able to bask in the reflected glory of an army whose steady overall improvement in performance had been accelerated by some spectacular and unexpected victories in Europe and further afield, although it could not be denied that successes were often dependent upon assistance from allies and foreign troops. The exploits of the army excited great interest and captured the public's imagination, and successful officers were hailed as national heroes in a manner that had hitherto been reserved only for popular naval commanders, such as Admiral Vernon (Wilson, 1988; Jordan and Rogers, 1989). This undoubtedly played its part in casting the army in a much more favourable light, even though its enhanced reputation was later tarnished as a result of the loss of America. In overall terms, and in spite of the setback of the early 1780s and a poor performance between 1793 and 1795, the army was widely represented in a much more positive fashion in the early nineteenth century than it had been a hundred years earlier. In large part, this was because it was seen as having made a vital contribution to the processes which underpinned the extraordinary improvement that had taken place in Britain's military and imperial fortunes.

A warlike people? Attitudes towards war

Changing attitudes towards the army should not be taken as an indication that the British were necessarily becoming a more militaristic, or warlike, people. There were many occasions when calls to arms were not answered promptly, or enthusiastically, by the population at large. Complaints about the county quota system caused widespread resistance to militia service in England and Wales after 1757, and recruitment drives by the army or navy often provoked violence and civil disorder (Western, 1965: 290–303; Boshedt, 1982: 172–84; Jenkins, 1987: 330; Stevenson, 1992: 46–51, 208–12). Small-scale clashes between civilians and naval press gangs or army recruiting parties were commonplace throughout the period, and in 1794 London was shaken by the 'anti-crimp' riots which represented a violent protest against the methods used by private recruiting agents and contractors who operated on the army's behalf (Stevenson, 1971). More often than not, however, these popular responses can be attributed to the perceived iniquities of specific recruiting tactics used by the authorities rather than to anti-war sentiment as such and, in general, public support for war very much depended upon who the enemy was and what form any intended action was to take. The com-

mencement of hostilities and the subsequent conduct of any campaigns usually prompted vigorous expressions of public sentiment,
and these were often very much shaped by the way in which pas-
sions had been inflamed by pro- or anti-ministerial sentiment and
by the general cut-and-thrust of domestic political debate. At
times, this could mean that support for government action was far
from unanimous.

Anti-war sentiment was evident, for example, during the War of
American Independence, when government actions were depicted
in some quarters as an unjustifiable attack upon the rights and
freedoms of fellow British subjects. Indeed, the political tempera-
ture was raised to the point that some senior officers refused to
serve against the colonists. Before the intervention of France and
Spain on behalf of the colonists in 1778 and 1779 respectively, the
nation was deeply divided over the issue. Rival groups in counties
and boroughs across the country sought to make representations
to king and Parliament in support of, or in opposition to, the coer-
cive action being taken against the colonists. Tensions ran so high
during the war that there were outbreaks of urban violence and
disorder, especially when opponents of the government chose not
to participate in 'patriotic' celebrations of victories (Wilson, 1995:
238–52; Colley, 1992: 137–41).

A similar polarisation of political opinion was evident during
the 1790s, when divisions between conservatives and loyalists on
one hand and radical reformers, republicans, and the 'Friends of
Peace' on the other, were sharpened by the emotions and fears
released by the outbreak of war against Revolutionary France.
Faced with the potentially dangerous combination of political
unrest at home and the triumph of French Revolutionary ideals on
the Continent, the government moved swiftly to clamp down on
sedition and disorder. This occurred as early disaffection with the
war moved beyond petitioning activity and the holding of mass
meetings to sporadic violent disturbances and attacks on the king
and those in positions of authority (Cookson, 1982; Wells, 1986;
Stevenson, 1992: 212–19). Repressive action, which in its first
phase included the introduction of the so-called 'Gagging Acts'
(the Treasonable and Seditious Practices Act and the Seditious
Meetings Act) of 1795 and the temporary suspensions of Habeas
Corpus in 1794 and 1795, took place against a background in

which anti-radical opinion was strengthened through the attempts made by the political and religious establishment to foster and organise popular patriotism and loyalism. In the long run, this helped to ensure the survival of the established order and the preservation of the constitution, while, at the same time, it allowed an increasingly united home front to be presented against the French (Christie, 1982: 213–29; Emsley, 1985; O'Gorman, 1989). This solidarity was strengthened further after 1803 when the war against Napoleon proved to be far more popular than the struggle against Revolutionary France.

Attitudes to war had been rather different, and public opinion had been far less divided, however, when great-power conflicts had been fought along clear-cut dynastic and religious lines without the constitutional or ideological complications present in the wars against the American colonists or Revolutionary France. When bellicose attention had been focused solely upon Britain's traditional European rivals, public support for wars was far more united and vociferous. Indeed, at times public opinion ran a long way ahead of cautious politicians and ministers. This was most notably the case in 1739, when there was great public excitement and celebration as concerted pressure from the merchant community helped to move the unpopular Walpole ministry towards a declaration of war against Spain (Wilson, 1995: 141–2). Successes against France and Spain were widely acclaimed, none more so than during the Seven Years' War, when heroes such as Amherst, Boscawen and Wolfe were canonised and victories were celebrated in bouts of enthusiastic public rejoicing across the country. Later in the century, success in a far-distant war fought by the East India Company against Tipu Sultan of Mysore was acclaimed as a national triumph, and the Governor-General of India, Lord Cornwallis (who earlier in his career had surrendered to the Americans at Yorktown) was widely fêted as a popular hero (Marshall, 1992). On the other hand, politicians and military commanders could pay a heavy price for embarrassing British failures when the public mood was set against an unpopular administration or the unsuccessful conduct of war. Lord George Sackville, the 'coward' of Minden, was publicly humiliated before the army in 1759, but he was fortunate by comparison with the luckless Admiral Byng, who was burnt in effigy across the country and then executed on board his flagship after a court martial which followed the loss of Minorca in 1756 (Wilson, 1995: 180–1).

The nature of these public responses to the struggle against the Bourbon powers saw expression being given to a wide range of intense loyal, patriotic and xenophobic sentiments which helped to forge a sense of national solidarity (Wilson, 1995: 197–8). The frequency and length of war ensured that, over time, these attitudes became deeply embedded in popular consciousness, and this helped to redefine what Britons thought about themselves and their place in the world. In particular, recurrent warfare played an important part in helping to establish a sense of common identity among the different people that had been brought into the United Kingdom following the Act of Union of 1707 between England and Scotland. As Linda Colley has argued in a recent influential study, the emergent British nation 'was an invention forged by war'. It became a nation 'used to fighting' and it 'largely defined itself through fighting' (Colley, 1992: 5, 9). Tensions long remained evident in relations between the English and their near-neighbours, but the diversion of martial energies and political attention into Europe and the wider world to meet the challenge posed by Catholic France and Spain helped to bring the Scots and Welsh together under the same Protestant banner as the English. Over time, this enabled a form of British identity to be superimposed upon long-standing regional and national loyalties, helping to reinforce the economic and political unity underpinning the foundations of the modern state. Britons everywhere, especially the elite, were able to define their identity, behaviour, lifestyles and virtues through comparison with the very different and, so it was held, greatly inferior characteristics displayed by the French. War repeatedly served to emphasise the fundamental differences that existed between Britain and the Bourbon powers, and in particular France, and this allowed Britons to establish at least some degree of common ground between one another (Colley, 1992).

Looking beyond public responses to different wars or types of conflict, it is possible to discern signs in some quarters of the beginnings of a shift in attitude towards war as an institution. This was by no means a widespread movement and the weight of opposing forces and influences was considerable. By the mid-eighteenth century, what has recently been described as the 'contemporary fascination' with war was being reinforced by the popular belief that success or failure in arms reflected divine judgement upon the moral state of the nation. Following on from this, it was widely felt that inherent British (and Protestant) strengths and virtues would reveal themselves in times of war (Harris, 1996: 118–20). Contemplation of these matters helped to sustain the notion that war was 'just' or righteous, and the Church played an important part in sustaining successive war efforts, not least through its mobilisation of popular support on days of public fasting and thanksgiving (Langford, 1989: 622–3). Nevertheless, in spite of the seal of religious approval given to British military activity by the established church throughout the eighteenth century, some were beginning to question the way in which war was so regularly used as a means of solving disputes between nations. Others recoiled from the horrors and consequences of modern conflict, and these sentiments, fuelled by a general weariness, multiplied during the Napoleonic war. Signs of an emerging pacifism are evident from the 1730s, and these took on a much firmer shape in the form of the peace 'movement' that emerged at the beginning of the nineteenth century (Ceadel, 1996: 65–7, 151–221; Cookson, 1982). By 1815, many Britons were no longer prepared fatalistically to resign themselves to the fact that a semi-permanent state of war was either necessary or inevitable.

It cannot be denied that war and military activity left a heavy imprint on the eighteenth-century British state and society. This is not to say, however, that Britain ever became a military state. There were certainly many political and institutional checks upon military and naval influence which served to prevent Britain becoming a state of the Austrian or Prussian type. Consequently, many of society's internal structures and relationships were never organised on *permanent* military lines as elsewhere in Europe, but none the less they were flexible and effective enough to keep the nation on a war footing for much of the time. This meant that long-term success could be achieved without ever it being felt necessary or desirable to sacrifice the defining features of civil society to the cause of militarism or to the development of a state driven entirely by the needs and wishes of its army and navy.

5
The wartime economy

The frequency, scale and changing nature of eighteenth-century warfare was such that much depended upon how the British economy was able to cope with the military demands imposed upon it. The performance of an expanding army and navy was determined to a considerable degree by the efficiency of domestic production and supply systems and, without reasonable levels of support from industry, agriculture and commerce, Britain's military efforts would have been seriously weakened. As such, different sectors within the economy were required to respond to the various challenges of war by producing a wide range of goods and materials of sufficient quantity and adequate quality to enable the armies of Britain and its allies to fight lengthy campaigns in Europe and the wider world. Moreover, because of the disruption caused by war to international trade and commerce, there was also a need for the domestic economy, especially the agricultural sector, to support the basic needs of an expanding population. Any analysis of the relationship between war and the domestic economy must, however, be set within much broader terms of reference than those which see economic activity as simply an important factor contributing to the state's military performance. During the eighteenth century, Britain began to be transformed by the various processes associated with industrialisation, and, in seeking to chart and explain the course of these changes, historians have identified war as exerting a powerful influence over the development of the domestic economy. For the purposes of this chapter, therefore, it will be necessary to examine the different economic effects of war before considering whether, on balance, they should be represented in positive or negative terms.

The economic impact of war

War represented only one of a number of factors influencing the general course of eighteenth-century economic activity. By interacting with, and often exacerbating, the effects of harvest failures, financial crises and the like, semi-continuous warfare ensured that the conditions for economic development in Britain were often far from perfect or stable. Fear of international conflict was enough to cause domestic depression, and war itself fuelled inflation and distorted patterns of demand within the economy (Cole, 1981: 52–4). Thus, the economy moved to an uncertain rhythm arising from the quite different circumstances that prevailed in wartime and postwar periods of varying lengths, and this ensured that full recovery from one conflict was seldom achieved before another commenced. The effects of this were acutely felt by the individuals who experienced food shortages, inflation, higher taxes and dislocations within the labour market. Not surprisingly, this led to war in general, and the Revolutionary and French wars in particular, depressing the nation's living standards (Mokyr and Savin, 1976).

In addition, specific wartime crises could also have severe and long-lasting economic consequences. Such was the case in 1797 when a small French invasion force landed near Fishguard in West Wales. This enemy action was ill fated, but it nevertheless triggered widespread panic and confusion. It caused a run on the banks, prompting the Bank of England to suspend cash payments, a decision which, in effect, took Britain off the gold standard. In response to the acute shortage of specie caused by this emergency action, new paper-money-issuing institutions were established across the country as attempts were made to ensure that routine economic activity could continue. The effects of this monetary reconstruction were so great that the economic historian J. H. Clapham was moved to declare that the war years could be described as 'the age of the bank notes' (Clapham, 1944, II: 4). The full resumption of cash payments did not take place until 1821 which meant that, as far as most people were concerned, a gradual and uncertain adjustment had to be made to new and often very difficult exchange conditions.

Yet, for all the obvious problems associated with an economy that was moving in a series of war-induced fits and starts, Britain's domestic experiences were quite different from those of its main rivals. In particular, unlike its European counterparts, Britain did not suffer from the destructive effects of military activity on its own soil. The general thrust of British strategy and, in particular, the effective deployment of naval resources throughout the period, ensured that the nation's economic infrastructure and institutions remained intact. This meant not only that the capital tied up in plant and goods was, for the most part, never seriously threatened by enemy action, but that Britain's basic patterns of economic development were quite different from those experienced by the European states whose territories acted as hosts to repeated and extensive military campaigns. In the very broadest terms, therefore, the relationship between war and British economic development must be defined in a context in which military power was used, in a consistently hostile world, to provide reasonable levels of long-term domestic security. War might have been expensive and unwelcome to many but, at the very least, the successful defence of the realm helped to establish a framework in which economic progress could still be made (O'Brien, 1993).

Although British industries and enterprises were reasonably well protected from the threat of physical damage or destruction by enemy forces, warfare nevertheless exerted a direct and profound influence upon patterns of growth and development in all sectors of the economy. War might be held to have retarded growth, for example, because it could quite clearly damage trade, distort patterns of domestic demand, and disrupt the labour market. Yet, in each of these cases, necessary and often painful readjustments were made and, over time, war could also begin to act as an influence that helped to sustain growth and development. To take the first case referred to above, British command of the seas meant that although wars, especially the early part of each conflict, were extremely disquieting times for many merchants, foreign trade continued to grow throughout the period. New opportunities presented themselves to merchants who were able and willing to diversify their activities, and military and naval success ensured that hitherto unexploited parts of the world were opened for the first time to British commercial influence. Throughout the period a large number of important colonial markets were gained at the expense of France, Holland and Spain. Again, as in the second case, consumer spending and activity in the building and construction trades might always have been reduced in wartime, but war also served to stimulate those industries which supplied the materials and equipment needed by the armed forces. Finally, the movement of large numbers of men into the armed forces was often accompanied by complaints, especially in rural areas and from the merchant shipping community, about the scarcity of labour, but this does not seem, in the long run, to have had a debilitating effect upon many forms of industrial economic activity. For the most part, wartime civilian manpower shortages were made good by the use of those who had hitherto been unemployed, and, as has been discussed, it was in post-war periods rather than during war itself that the problems associated with a badly dislocated workforce were most acutely felt. Each of these examples suggest that no simple calculation of benefit, or cost, may be applied to the wartime experience of any one sector within the economy. Not only do setbacks suffered in one context have to be reconciled with advances made elsewhere, but it has to be acknowledged that, over time, fortunes fluctuated wildly across, and within, different areas of activity.

War and industrialisation: the historical debate

Confronted by many obvious signs of distress and dislocation around them, most contemporary observers assumed that war inflicted great damage upon the British economy. The assessments made by historians have not always been so gloomy, though, because hindsight suggests that the economy was able to derive important strength from adversity. Indeed, some have argued that although repeated transitions from peace to war, and back, caused serious dislocations and discontinuities within the economy, they also allowed Britain to advance in the long run on a number of different fronts. This was because, over time, circumstances dictated that an 'unintended balance' was achieved between those economic sectors that were driven primarily by the demands of war and those that were not (Langford, 1989: 636). Others, however, have noted that any attempt to come to a general, or balanced, conclusion about the overall effects of war upon the British economy is a well-nigh impossible task. This is because a formidable weight of evidence can be assembled to support the view that international conflict served both to retard and promote development (Deane, 1975: 91). Of course, in many ways this is a problem that can never be fully and satisfactorily resolved. On the one hand, the historian is faced with the difficult task of isolating the effects of war from other important factors that influenced British economic development. On the other hand, there is also a need to enter the realm of counterfactual speculation in an attempt to determine what might have happened to the domestic economy if Britain had not been at war for much of the period under review. Moreover, at each stage of the analytical process, elements of real doubt and uncertainty are introduced into any calculation, or hypothesis, for the simple reason that the reconstruction of what actually happened to the British economy has to be based upon statistical data which is often limited and fragmentary in its nature. Nevertheless, in spite of all these difficulties, historians have attempted over many years to offer appraisals of the impact of war upon the economy and they have arrived at a variety of quite different general conclusions.

During the 1950s, T. S. Ashton declared in unequivocal terms that war had a negative effect upon the development of the economy during the long eighteenth century. The smooth running of business and industry was repeatedly disrupted, he argued, as labour and resources were diverted away from peaceful and socially beneficial enterprises such as building and construction into activities that were driven by the acute needs of war (Ashton, 1959: 49–83). This meant that the development of the economy was interrupted at regular intervals, and the effects were such that the very fabric of society was eroded and the material well-being of individuals was badly affected. Indeed, when Ashton chose to define the economic impact of war in these terms, he argued that warfare distorted economic activity to such a degree that 'If there had been no wars the English people would have been better fed, better clad, certainly better housed than they were.' Without eighteenth-century wars, he concluded, 'the Industrial Revolution might have come earlier' (Ashton, 1959: 83).

Others, however, applied quite different criteria, and the general tone of some of their conclusions has been rather more positive than those offered by Ashton. During the mid-1950s, for example,

A. H. John wrote that war 'exerted, on the whole, a beneficial influence on the economy' (John, 1955: 343). John confined his analysis to the period between 1700 and 1763, observing that war served to promote technological advances and created surges in demand for the products of the metallurgical and shipping industries. He also suggested that wartime conditions did not lead to major contractions in non-military economic activity, because domestic manpower resources were not heavily depleted by the armed forces. John was at pains to point out that his conclusions were not appropriate for the wars that followed, and, indeed, he briefly identified a number of 'counterbalancing factors' evident in the conflicts of the late eighteenth century. Others again have chosen to suggest that the negative economic effects evident during the most extensive and expensive wars of the period – the wars against Revolutionary and Napoleonic France – should not be overstated. Indeed, by the mid-1970s, Phyllis Deane was arguing that, although many matters remained unresolved, 'the accessible evidence taken as a whole does not support the view that the war of 1793–1815 exerted a serious brake on British industrial progress'. She concluded that the wars against Revolutionary and Napoleonic France did not cause 'more than superficial fluctuations in the pace and content of the British Industrial Revolution' (Deane, 1975: 100–1). Anderson in fact went one step further than this and declared that the same wars seemed 'likely to have been conducive even fundamental to British economic growth in the period 1783–1815' (Anderson, 1972: 18).

The views outlined above represent significant disagreements among historians about the general economic effects of warfare and, although much clearly depends on the different criteria used to measure progress, controversy continues to characterise debate about British economic development during the French and Napoleonic wars in particular. Over the last twenty years, a great number of detailed studies on the late eighteenth-century economy have appeared, and the analysis and reworking of statistical data have allowed historians to reassess the positive and negative economic effects of those wars. Some, perhaps quite rightly, still adopt a position in the middle ground, from where they draw attention to a range of wartime costs and benefits, and to the unevenness of the impact of the war across time and different sectors (Crouzet, 1989: 207–8). Others, though, especially the 'new' economic historians, have produced quantitative analyses which have opened up marked differences of opinion over the general long-term effects of the war upon the British economy.

The stimulus for much of this debate was provided by Williamson, who developed an argument based upon the claim that the several effects of war were such that British rates of growth and industrialisation were significantly lower than they might otherwise have been between 1790 and 1820, the period located at the heart of the classically formulated Industrial Revolution (Williamson, 1984). Williamson's work helped breathe new life into discussion about British industrialisation, and a series of vigorous exchanges have occurred as his conclusions and methods have been subjected to close scrutiny. Although many differences of opinion can never be fully resolved, it is worth stressing that Williamson's counterfactual calculations of possible growth in peacetime – the 'what might have been' – have been criticised for producing estimates that are too high. In addition, it has been argued that he has overstated the negative effects upon rates of private capital accumulation and investment caused by the 'crowding out' that occurred when the government stepped up its wartime search for savings to borrow (Crafts, 1987; Mokyr, 1987; O'Brien, 1989a).

Although critics of Williamson have not denied that, in the absence of war, rates of growth would have been greater than those achieved, it has been argued in recent years that the wartime experience did not necessarily serve to damage the nation's interests or undermine its overall economic strength. Analysis based upon a combination of revised estimates for key growth indicators and sector-by-sector analysis of industry suggests that although 'on average the rate of growth for industrial production proceeded more rapidly during the 1780s and 1820s and 1830s than it did during the war', the experiences of major industries were such that only a few (notably brewing, building and distilling) were adversely affected by wartime conditions (O'Brien, 1989a: 360–4; Crouzet, 1989: 199–202). It has even been suggested that the industrial revolution 'occurred precisely during and because of the Napoleonic wars' (Neal, 1990: 218). Standing Williamson's argument on its head, Neal has claimed that at times between 1793 and 1815

Britain's wartime economy experienced 'crowding in' rather than 'crowding out' as capital took flight from war-torn Europe and was put to good use in government funds (especially the 3 per cent consols) and elsewhere. He argues that, finding itself 'locked in' to Britain by Napoleon's continental blockade, some of this capital then found its way into productive investment in industry and the nation's economic infrastructure (Neal, 1990: 180–222). There is much that is extremely tentative about such a conclusion (as there is with so many others), but it does illustrate that assessments of the effects of war upon the industrialisation process are not as negative as they once were.

Moving on from general to specific issues, it is now necessary to consider three important aspects of the relationship between war and British economic development. These are, first, the various ways in which government policy on taxation and spending affected the wider economy; second, the question of whether war acted as a spur to innovation, invention and technological change; and, finally, the domestic consequences of wartime disruptions to overseas trade and commerce.

Government and the wartime economy

In the very broadest of terms, eighteenth-century warfare helped to establish the general framework within which all aspects of economic development occurred. This was because the effects of government wartime funding strategies were felt throughout the economy at large, and they helped to regulate the ebb and flow of trade, commerce, agriculture and industry. In acknowledging the importance of this, it has been argued that the form taken by the state's financial policies, notably during the wars of 1793–1815, help to explain why rates of economic growth in Britain slowed after 1780. In particular, it has been held that increased levels of government borrowing 'crowded out' private investment in industry and productive activity at a critical moment in the nation's economic development, and this served to limit capital formation and growth (Williamson, 1984). Such an argument focuses attention on the need to consider government wartime policies not simply in terms of their effectiveness in raising the finance necessary to meet the French threat, but also in terms of the general influences they exerted within and upon the domestic economy. It has already been noted that the burden of taxation imposed upon the British population was a heavy one, which exerted considerable influence upon levels of demand and investment within the economy. More specifically, because successive governments pursued a fairly consistent policy of raising additional revenue from indirect taxes, notably the Excise, this fiscal strategy served, of course, to regulate the consumption and manufacture of domestically produced goods.

There are, however, two ways of looking at this strategy. The emphasis on indirect rather than direct tax seems to have had the effect of reducing demand for goods and building activity, and this might well have served to apply a brake to some aspects of the industrialisation process (Beckett and Turner, 1990). On the other hand, it can also be argued that the government's financial strategy helped, in the longer term, to sustain industrialisation, especially during the crucial years of the French wars at the end of the period. Then, governments continued to find the funds for the prosecution of war from loans and taxation but, in a break with tradition, almost 60 per cent of the additional funds raised for military spending came from the latter source (Mathias and O'Brien, 1976: 623; O'Brien, 1988: 4). Against a fiscal background in which the emphasis of the tax burden continued to be placed upon consumption rather than wealth or savings (in spite of the introduction of income tax in 1799), it seems that, in the words of O'Brien, 'Investment was restrained but not "crowded out" by the Government's heavy demands for loanable funds' (O'Brien, 1989a: 347). This view is supported by some analyses of the relationship between state borrowing and general interest rate behaviour (Heim and Mirowski, 1987), although historians remain divided over the issue of whether or not the government's search for funds did in fact serve to cause a 'lagged' crowding out effect through the eventual forcing up of interest rates (Black and Gilmore, 1990). In any event, although private consumption fell quite sharply – from 83 per cent of national expenditure in 1788–92 to 64 per cent by 1815 – the share of national income devoted to investment remained fairly constant throughout the French wars (O'Brien, 1989a: 347). Seen in this light, although Pitt's move away from a government financial strategy based largely upon borrowing was not founded upon any predetermined master plan (O'Brien 1989b), it was, in practice, an important and sensible decision. It restrained the further growth of the National Debt and avoided drawing upon a pool of resources and savings that could still be applied to private investment.

The outcome of this strategy was that, although house building was hard hit at times, key areas of activity such as canal and road construction, and the cotton and iron industries, were not starved of funds because actual or potential investors were taking flight in order to seek better rates of return on loans made to government. Rather, as seems to have been the case throughout the period (Dickson and Sperling, 1971; Lee, 1986: 68), increased levels of government borrowing were based upon the investment of 'idle' funds, not funds that would otherwise have found their way into agriculture, commerce, or industry (Anderson, 1972: 7–9). These idle funds were held by domestic public creditors who, in the main, lived in London and the South East of England (Dickson, 1967: 249–303). They represented a section of the investing community who operated in a capital market that was quite different in structure and form from that which supported the world of industrial finance. There are few, if any, signs of manufacturing firms being starved of funds during this period (Cottrell, 1980: 1–16), and in the long run it seems that warfare did not seriously depress levels of private investment (O'Brien, 1994). The existence of separate and parallel markets helped to ensure that there was no acute shortage of funds for either government borrowing or private investment, and Pitt's recasting of government funding and taxation strategy during the late 1790s managed, intentionally or not, to strike a careful balance between the needs of the state and those of the private sector. The Excise undoubtedly bore very heavily upon rates of consumption of some domestic goods such as glass, paper, coal, candles and the products of the brewing industry, but the selective use of indirect taxation ensured that the textile, pottery and metallurgical industries, as well as the banking, insurance and shipping services, often escaped lightly or altogether (Hudson, 1992: 55).

Throughout the period, much of the government finance raised by taxation and borrowing was fed back into the economy as military expenditure of one type or another. Of course, some of the funds that were essential for the war effort were written off or lost altogether because they were diverted into subsidies for allies, wages for mercenaries, or dividend payments to foreign stock-holders. At times, as we have seen with regard to subsidies, these losses could be quite substantial. However, the British government's procurement of domestic goods and services was considerable, and it has been estimated that between 1688 and 1815 over 80 per cent of public expenditure was dedicated to purchasing for military purposes (O'Brien, 1993: 135). Although there are considerable methodological and analytical problems associated with estimating the overall effect of government expenditure upon British economic growth (Jackson, 1990), this nevertheless represented a significant government-directed reallocation of resources within the economy, and it strengthened the position of favoured firms and suppliers. Wartime government orders for the goods necessary to meet the requirements of the army and navy stimulated demand across a range of industries – from armaments and gunpowder, through metallurgy and shipbuilding to clothing and shoes, foodstuffs and fodder. Indeed, the importance of this is revealed by the way in which the Navy Victualling Office became one of the nation's largest purchasers of agricultural produce (Duffy, 1980: 78). At the same time, the need to procure, transport, and deliver necessary items, especially provisions, for the armed forces created considerable business opportunities for those wealthy and well-connected merchants who were granted supply contracts by the Treasury Board (Baker, 1971).

The volume of goods required by the armed forces of Britain and its allies was large and it increased as the nature of warfare changed during the period. Partly in response to this, partly to ensure greater levels of quality control, and partly to reduce dependence on private contractors, the state began to become more deeply involved in the production process. The Board of Ordnance exercised close supervision over the manufacture of firearms from 1715; brass founding and gun boring began at Woolwich in 1716; and in 1759 the government purchased its own gunpowder mills at Haversham (Houlding, 1981: 137–8; West, 1991: 149–66). There was also a steady increase in the number of men working in the royal dockyards during wartime – a rise from just under 6,500 in 1711 to over 15,500 in 1814 – and this helped to ensure that the yards became some of the most important centres of industrial activity in the country (Coad, 1989: 1–21). Even so, for the most part the state still had to rely upon private firms to produce gunpowder and military and naval equipment. Lucrative wartime openings existed for those who possessed skills and facilities that were in short supply and, early in the period, whenever the royal dockyards could not build ships fast enough to meet wartime naval demand, orders were placed with private yards (Coleman, 1953: 153; Ehrman, 1953: 88). By the time of the War of Austrian Succession, private yards were building most of the navy's smaller vessels, while the royal dockyards concentrated their attention on repairs, refits, and the more specialised construction of large ships (Baugh, 1965: 241–6).

Nevertheless, not all manufacture and supply problems could be solved by a division of labour between public and private enterprise, and the successful conduct of military operations still ran the risk of being hampered by production and supply difficulties when specialised manufacturers were placed under acute pressure. This happened during the Seven Years' War, most notably in 1761–2, when serious problems were caused by significant shortfalls in the availability of gunpowder and weapons (West, 1991; Black, 1994b: 55–7). Gradually, however, the situation improved. Sustained experience of wartime conditions enabled producers of military goods and equipment to refine the techniques and procedures necessary for them to increase productive capacity as and when required, even though their basic methods often remained firmly rooted in traditional practices and procedures. This, together with the building up of reserve stores, meant that, in terms of quantity if not always of quality, an adequate supply of weapons was available to Britain and its allies by the end of the period. Britain produced well over 3,000,000 small arms between 1793 and 1815, and, by the end of the war against Napoleon, there were almost three-quarters of a million muskets in store (Black, 1994b: 57).

Although it is possible to identify several industries, such as armaments and shipbuilding, which derived a great deal of direct benefit from sustained warfare, economic historians have tended to stress that the effects of increased government-led wartime demand were only narrowly felt within the manufacturing sector. Most have been rather cautious in their assessment of the overall effects of government spending within the economy at large, and one historian has concluded that 'war-time demand ... had not assumed such dimensions as to gear the whole economy to its priorities' (Birch 1967: 52). It should be pointed out, however, that there are a few exceptions to this general rule. McNeill, for example, argued that government spending for military purposes 'profoundly affected' the 'absolute volume of production and the mix of products' generated between 1793 and 1815, and, rather less emphatically, Anderson declared that government demand offered 'a continuing, though declining support for the economy' (McNeill, 1983: 211; Anderson, 1974: 616). Indeed, the procurement of supplies and the basic raw materials by those who manufactured goods for the army and navy must have had a stimulating effect upon associated trades and industries. Military orders could, for example, represent significant demand for a variety of agricultural products because fodder, foodstuffs and livestock were always required in large quantities. Similarly, clothing and shoes contracts brought great benefit to sections of the agricultural community. Orders, such as the one placed for the monthly supply of 638,000 pairs of shoes between April and December 1811, offered a considerable boost to farmers who supplied those working in the leather trade (Clarkson, 1989: 469; Perren, 1989: 201). At an individual or local level, many other similar links and wartime flows of goods can be established, but it remains difficult if not impossible to calculate precisely how much the growth of any one sector might be ascribed to demand generated by government agencies.

Where reasonably reliable quantitative data have been assembled and analysed, the effects of military demand upon key industries do not always point to unambiguous conclusions and allow for the emergence of a consensus view among historians. This is the case, for example, with the iron industry whose products were used for cannon boring and the manufacture of small arms, shot and shells. At an individual level, leading iron masters secured many military and naval orders from abroad as well as home during wartime, and some undoubtedly generated great profits (Ashton, 1951: 130–2; Flinn, 1962: 147–70). As a consequence, the development of some of the largest industrial enterprises in the country, such as the Carron Company works in Scotland and the furnaces built by Richard Crawshay and his various associates around the village of Merthyr in South Wales, was driven to a considerable extent by the demand for iron from the Board of Ordnance (Campbell, 1961; Evans, 1993: 10–29). Yet in overall terms, it has been estimated that the combined weight of government purchases accounted for only just under 20 per cent of total iron output during the 1790s and 1800s (Hyde, 1977: 115; Harris, 1988: 55; Birch, 1967: 52), and that only around 10 per cent of additional output of the 'primary branch' of the iron industry was used for military purposes between 1793 and 1815 (Crouzet, 1989: 200). It has been argued that the major dynamics of expansion were to be found in the development of bigger and better furnaces, and in other, war-related, factors such as the introduction of Cort's puddling process and improvements in Britain's international trading position; but government orders were undoubtedly important to an industry whose annual pig iron output rose from 70,000 to 395,000 tons and whose bar iron output increased from 32,000 tons to 150,000 tons between 1788 and 1815 (Hyde, 1977: 112–15). That this was so might be surmised from the immediate post-war situation faced by the industry which, in spite of increasing levels of iron exports, experienced hard times and falling output as government orders for weapons and military equipment decreased (Hyde, 1977: 135–40). Indeed, pig iron ouput did not return to the level of 1815 until 1821 or 1822 (Hyde 1977: 135; Riden, 1977: 455).

Warfare, innovation, and technological change

If economic historians are rather cautious about the effect of military demand upon the growth of particular industries, they are also inclined to play down the role of warfare as an agent of change and improvement within the industrial sectors of the economy. This is not to deny that war played some part in stimulating innovation in general. It is quite clear, for example, that government wartime expenditure on the navy helped to improve the performance of ships as well as sailing techniques (O'Brien, 1991: 20). Moreover, as has been shown, many of the important developments associated with public finance and the rise of the stock market emerged as a by-product of the state's need to channel the nation's resources into military spending. And in an altogether different field, the positive effects of hospital and preventive practices, first introduced in the army and navy, were later felt throughout civil society (Mathias, 1979: 264–85). However, in the key area of technology, which lay close to the heart of Britain's industrial transformation, there are few signs that war promoted widespread change either in terms of the introduction of new weapons or in the manufacture of equipment and goods destined for the armed forces.

In the early part of the period, war years were always accompanied by the submission of large numbers of military inventions to government departments (Macleod, 1988: 35–6), but these had little effect on the way that war was conducted. Most advances represented improvements (often copied from rival powers) to existing systems rather than departures into new types of weapons or equipment. Prototype models of new weapons usually failed to advance beyond the testing stage, and inventors were often frustrated by a combination of inadequate development facilities and a conservative military establishment which, for the most part, remained firmly wedded to the tried and trusted ways of warfare. The rockets designed by William Congreve and introduced with some success during the Napoleonic war were an exception to this general rule (Black, 1994b: 44–60).

As far as the production process itself was concerned, the need to provide large quantities of equipment, goods and weapons for the armed forces did act in some way as a spur to the use of new technology. The shipbuilding and ship repair industries provide several examples, late in the period, of innovation serving to enhance productive capacity and efficiency. The *general* effects of this should not be overstated, however, because the most commonly cited technological developments were not found in regular use beyond the royal dockyards. For many years, these dockyards were themselves regarded by historians as being inefficient and incompetently managed agencies which did little to help the cause of the navy but recent work has contributed to the painting of a much more favourable picture. During the 1790s, over three-quarters of the navy's ships of the line and frigates were in commission (French, 1990: 92), and a detailed study concludes that the 'Navy was remarkably well served by its building and repair policies' (Webb, 1988). Indeed, it is now argued that, by the end of the Napoleonic war, a commitment to reform and the introduction of new techniques and technology had combined to transform the yards into operations characterised by 'industry, enterprise, and gradual improvement' (Morriss, 1983: 9). In large part, the reform measures that prompted this transformation were inspired by Samuel Bentham, who was the Inspector General of Naval Works between 1796 and 1805. As part of his strategy, he oversaw the introduction of machinery designed to improve efficiency and speed up the building and repair process. Technical innovations included the introduction of block-making machinery designed by Marc Brunel and, after 1799, the use of steam engines to drive pumps, lathes and saws. At the same time, an assembly line was established at Deptford to facilitate the manufacture of large numbers of ships' biscuits (Morriss, 1983; Coad, 1989). The combined weight of these reforms in large-scale industrial enterprises was such that one historian has been moved to remark that the dockyards were 'as much in the forefront of the industrialisation process as were the civilian textile mills' (Emsley, 1979: 108–9).

Even though the dockyards were prepared, under the pressures of international conflict, to adopt some 'state of the art' labour-saving devices, it should not be assumed that, in general terms, war helped to facilitate the widespread diffusion of the new ideas and methods related to the processes associated with industrialisation and modernisation. Some key war-related industries remained largely unaffected by technological change and, for example, a great deal of armament manufacture continued to be located in small workshops where production techniques remained crude and unsophisticated (Black, 1994b: 52). Furthermore, there was only a limited transfer of innovation from the military to the civilian industrial sectors during the period although, notably, John Wilkinson's cannon lathe device did prove itself capable of boring the cylinders required by James Watt's steam engine. In general, not many 'spin-offs' of a widely applicable practical type emerged from the manufacturing activity that was dedicated to the support of the British armed forces (Trebilcock, 1969). War might have encouraged the 'take up' of some new technology by the army and navy, and those who supplied them, but it failed to act as a general catalytic agent of mechanical and scientific progress. As far as British industry as a whole was concerned, little tangible benefit was derived by way of a return on the nation's considerable wartime expenditure.

An economy under siege: trade and agriculture

Analyses of commercial statistics do not suggest that the overall progress of Britain's foreign trade was arrested to any great degree by war during the eighteenth century (indeed growth rates accelerated after *c*.1740), but they do indicate that expansion was always interrupted during periods of international conflict, most notably during the War of American Independence (Deane and Cole, 1969: 45–50; Thomas and McCloskey, 1981: 88–90). Thus, although the figures representing the long-term growth of English and British trade are on the face of it impressive (a 5.2-fold increase in the value of imports, a 5.7-fold increase in the value of exports, and a 9-fold increase in the value of re-exports between 1700 and 1800), they conceal the fact that this growth usually moved to a rhythm marked by sharp contractions during the early years of wartime, subsequent recovery, and then the release of pent up demand on the return of peace. This pattern helped to ensure that, because the price of imports always rose in wartime and then fell upon the return of peace, the terms of trade tended to move against Britain during each conflict and in its favour after the cessation of hostilities (Deane and Cole, 1969: 85).

The uneven growth of foreign trade in difficult circumstances was dependent upon the actions and decisions of British merchants and manufacturers, many of whom were able to draw considerable strength from the military and naval successes which enabled them to develop a much wider range of commercial links across the world. Thus, for example, during the Seven Years' War, the seizing of commercial opportunities resulted in large quantities of goods being channelled into the newly captured territories of Canada, Cuba and Guadeloupe (Williams, 1972: 440–1; Peters, 1980: 150–1). Indeed, the opening of new trade outlets as a result of military victory and the acquisition of new territory at the negotiating table can be seen to have played an important part in ensuring that trade with the rest of the world eventually surpassed that with Europe (Thomas and McCloskey 1981: 90–3). As a result, Britain was never solely dependent upon one sector, trade or region and it gained a marked advantage over rivals such as France and Spain whose commercial interests were far narrower and could therefore be more easily damaged through the use of naval power in times of war. This was no more clearly underlined than during the Napoleonic war when, such was the stranglehold imposed upon Europe by British naval activity and blockading tactics, the imperial trading systems of France, Spain and Portugal were destroyed and the 'Atlantic sector' of the continental economy collapsed altogether (Crouzet, 1964). In such circumstances, Europe's losses were Britain's gains, and British merchants were able to establish, or re-establish, a range of commercial links with the Levant, the West Indies, Argentina, Brazil and other parts of the South American continent.

In view of the long-term growth of British overseas trade, it would clearly be inaccurate to suggest that commerce could not flourish during wartime, and much depended upon the navy's ability to secure command of the seas. It was often possible for the shipment of essential supplies to continue in key sectors during times of conflict (Kent, 1973), and this allowed for overall growth in British trade. Overseas trade expanded, for example, during the early part of the War of Spanish Succession (Jones, 1989: 169–210), although a significant depression set in thereafter (Deane and Cole, 1969: 49). It expanded again, and export values reached record levels, during the later stages of the Seven Years' War when, following the Battle of Quiberon Bay in 1759, the navy was able to confine much of the French fleet to port. Indeed, the merchant community's ability to adapt to wartime conditions and take advantage of Britain's military successes was such that, as far as exports were concerned, official aggregate values were always greater in the final year of wars than they were in the first (Hoppit, 1987: 99). Thus, even during the difficult years at the end of the eighteenth century and the beginning of the nineteenth century, the value of British exports increased steadily. Annual exports rose from an estimated value of £13.6 million in 1784–6, to £24.0 million in 1794–6, £41.2 million in 1804–6, and £48.0 million in 1814–16 (Davis, 1979: 86) and, as far as the composition of these exports was concerned, it was during the war years that cotton took on a larger form than woollen products within the commodity profile (Deane and Cole, 1969: 30–1).

It is important, however, that this impressive commercial performance in unfavourable circumstances should not be allowed to
divert attention away from the serious damage that was sometimes
inflicted upon British trade and industry during wartime. During
the Nine Years' War, for example, the pressures were such that the
navy was not able to offer adequate protection to shipping, and
consequently English and colonial merchants lost many valuable
cargoes (Jones, 1989: 145–61). In the case of the War of American
Independence, the textile trade was badly affected when British
merchants were denied access to important markets in the former
colonies and this caused a major recession in the domestic woollen
industry (Conway, 1995b: 190; Holderness, 1989: 120–1). Later,
during the wars against France, the export activity of the textile
industry in general was hard hit between 1808 and 1811 as the
effects of successive blockades were felt and then the American
market was closed to British merchants (Emsley, 1979: 136, 153).

The unpredictability of war caused much anxiety and uncertainty within the business community, and the normal calculations
of profitability were suspended as merchants were confronted by
the need to cover the higher operating costs incurred because of
increases in insurance and wage rates. For their part, although
masters and ship owners were able to double or even treble their
wartime freight rates, they often ran the very real risk of losing
their vessels. The extent of this risk, which added a great deal to the
normal hazards associated with overseas trade, is underlined by the
numbers of merchant vessels either destroyed or, more commonly,
held for ransom by the enemy. Although there are difficulties
involved in obtaining accurate assessments of merchant shipping
losses and captures in wartime, various contemporary and modern
estimates suggest that England lost around 4,000 ships between
1689 and 1697; at least 2,000 between 1702 and 1713; 3,000
between 1739 and 1748; and 3,386 between 1775 and 1783.
There are no figures or estimates available for losses incurred during the Seven Years' War, although the extent of British naval
supremacy over the French suggests that they were probably far
fewer than during other wars of the period. Even then, they were
probably not inconsiderable (Davis, 1962: 315–37). During the
French wars at the end of the period, 11,000 merchant vessels
were lost, together with cargoes valued at £62 million (O'Brien,

1989a: 339). These losses were keenly and widely felt within the business community and it is not surprising that, because of this and the other risks involved with trade, overseas merchants experienced higher levels of bankruptcy than any other section of eighteenth-century society (Hoppit, 1987: 96). Wartime always sent shock waves through the business world and it produced heavy casualty rates in the trade, banking and financial sectors (Joslin, 1960; Price and Clemens, 1987).

In response to the uncertainties of war, the merchant and shipping community sought better protection through the development of institutional and operational innovations which brought considerable long-term benefits to the maritime industry. For merchants who wished to remain committed to long-established trades and routes, some security was provided the increasing levels of protection offered by the Admiralty during the course of the eighteenth century. Convoys played an important part in ensuring that merchant shipping losses did not again reach the peak experienced during the Nine Years' War (Crowhurst, 1977). Not only were merchants' ships increasingly well protected after 1713, but those using the convoy system were favoured with better insurance rates than those who chose to go it alone. By the end of the period some convoys contained over 500 merchant vessels and twenty or more escorts. The need effectively to co-ordinate such a high level of shipping activity led, in turn, to a great degree of co-operation between the Admiralty and Lloyd's during the wars against Revolutionary and Napoleonic France. This, together with internal constitutional and managerial reform, helped to transform the position of Lloyd's in the world of marine insurance, and by 1815 the corporation had become firmly entrenched as a well-regarded and reliable institution at the heart of the City of London (Straus, 1937). At the same time, the logistical pressures created by the assembly of large convoys had a considerable impact upon the development of the Port of London, where wartime congestion in the Pool played an important part in helping to prompt the extensive dock-building activity that began during the 1790s (Stern, 1952). The overall effect of these changes helped, during a time of near-constant warfare, to facilitate a doubling in size of the British merchant fleet to over two and a half million tons between 1786 and 1815. Moreover, in response to the better provision of insurance, the same years also witnessed the emergence of the specialist sole owners of shipping alongside the older types of merchant investors and share owners who spread risks across several vessels (Ville, 1987).

Although trade was always one of the first victims of international conflict, British merchants were not affected by warfare in a uniformly harmful manner. Much depended upon the location of their home port because this determined their capacity to come to terms with the disruptions and uncertainties imposed by wartime conditions. Time and again, for example, Bristol's transatlantic trade was badly damaged by enemy maritime activity. This was reflected in significant reductions in the number of ships entering the port from transatlantic regions during war years and it had a considerable impact upon the nature and conduct of business within the city. Many merchants fell by the wayside, notably during the Seven Years' War, while others were forced to adapt in order to survive. Bristolians were swift to turn to privateering – the capture of ships and cargo from the enemy – but, although rich pickings could made, this could not disguise the fact that warfare was hindering the general advance and development of the port. Not only were contractions and expansions in the volume of trade influenced by patterns of war and recovery, but Bristol, as well as the smaller south-western ports of Barnstaple, Bideford, Exeter, and Plymouth, was unable to compete on equal terms with better-placed west coast rivals such as Liverpool and Glasgow. While Bristol merchants were taking heavy losses as their ships and cargoes fell prey to the French and Spanish in home waters and further afield, their counterparts in Liverpool and Glasgow were able to deploy vessels along transatlantic routes to the north of Ireland, and they made use of re-export passages to Europe around the north of Scotland that were relatively free from enemy activity. Moreover, at the return of peace Bristol merchants often found it difficult to recapture trade lost to their commercial rivals during war years. As a result, although the Atlantic trade continued to expand, Bristol found that it was losing ground to Glasgow in the tobacco trade, and to Liverpool in the slave trade. Both Liverpool and Glasgow were able to profit from Bristol's misfortune, and warfare can be identified as having played a part in both the relative commercial decline of Bristol and the broader restructuring that was occurring in Britain's transatlantic trade (Morgan, 1993: 11–32, 220–1; Price and Clemens, 1987).

More adventurous spirits who stayed in the world of maritime enterprise often found that wartime conditions offered entry into new types of business and enterprise. For some, government contracting and the leasing of ships offered a lucrative area of investment which softened any commercial blow caused by the commencement of hostilities. As noted above, privateering could also offer a richly rewarding form of wartime enterprise in the right circumstances. Operating within an increasingly well-regulated area of activity, albeit one that contained a large element of risk, a ship owner could receive a licence or 'letters of marque' from the authorities empowering him to seize and retain enemy vessels and goods. The prize would then be divided into shares between investors and the crew, the Crown having forsaken its claim to any proceeds in 1708. This offered the prospect, if not always the realisation, of rich pickings in home waters and much further afield, and those conducting well-organised and well-resourced privateering operations could at times secure an impressive rate of return on their initial capital outlay. Such activity attracted considerable numbers of participants who were prepared to invest in and man privateering vessels. During the War of Spanish Succession 1,343 vessels were licensed for privateering activity, and the number almost doubled to 2,676 between 1777 and 1783 when France and Spain joined the American colonists in their struggle against Britain (Starkey, 1990a). In 1779 it was estimated that around 9,000 men were at work on the 120 privateers operating out of Liverpool alone (Langford, 1989: 624). Privateering thus represented a considerable maritime enterprise, and, although it has been argued that it played only a marginal role in the overall development of the economy, it nevertheless enabled a significant number of entrepreneurs and seamen to come to terms with the disruption to normal commercial activity caused by war (Starkey, 1990a).

Whereas domestic industries, such as textiles, could be seriously damaged by the loss of overseas trading outlets, others drew great benefit and strength from the wartime reduction of foreign competition in domestic markets that followed from disruptions to supply and the imposition of tariffs designed to increase government revenue. In particular, the iron industry responded with some degree of success to the variety of circumstances that led to the reduction of foreign imports, and this was especially the case during the French wars of 1793 to 1815. Domestic iron producers, who had managed to capture only 60 per cent of the home market before 1790, were able to take advantage of wartime fiscal and commercial conditions to transform this situation after 1793, and by the beginning of the nineteenth century the British iron industry had become the strongest in Europe (Hyde, 1977: 114; Harris, 1988: 55).

The situation was rather different as far as agriculture was concerned because, while wartime usually witnessed increases in output, the nation was still dependent to some degree upon supplies of imported food and grain. This was especially so during the 1790s, when unprecedented levels of imported grain played a part in offsetting the worst effects of wartime harvest failure and food shortage. Although in some areas as much as three-quarters of local demand was being met by imported grain in 1800 (Wells, 1988: 194, 198), the overall figures suggest that only around 12 per cent of the population's need for wheat and flour was ever met by imports during the French wars (Hueckel, 1981: 184). The pressures on domestic agriculture that were associated with the combined effects of crop failure, increased demand from the armed forces, and dislocations in the labour market were thus exacerbated by the limits to importation that were imposed by disruptions to overseas trade and, during the Napoleonic period, the enemy's blockade. At times during the French wars of 1793 to 1815, and despite attempts by government to increase imports and encourage the use of alternative foodstuffs, estimates of national wheat deficiencies were considerable with, for example, the figure being put at 2 million quarters in December 1800 (Wells, 1988: 201). The need for British farmers to make good this significant deficit and allay fears of shortages by further increasing their output and productivity was made all the more urgent by the desire to sustain a population which rose steadily in number during the French wars.

In the particularly difficult circumstances of the early nineteenth century, British farmers and landlords responded to wartime conditions and sharply rising prices by increasing investment, and adopting new crops, livestock and agricultural practices. Moreover, as accelerating rates of parliamentary enclosure indicate, they also brought more acreage into use than ever before (Hueckel, 1982: 184–92). The wartime enclosure of common, wasteland and open field arable was considerable, and took cultivation into new and sometimes inhospitable parts of the country such as the Pennines. In total, between 1793 and 1813, there were 2,000 Acts of Enclosure affecting around 3 million acres, and private treaty brought about the same amount of land under cultivation (Turner, 1980; 1984). The effects of this, together with rises of productivity per acre, were felt after 1800 when the nation, although still importing some grain from Germany, Ireland, and North America, managed to meet almost nine-tenths of its needs in wheat and almost all of its needs in other grains (Christie, 1982: 161). It also seems likely that, although more acreage was brought under the plough, helping significantly to increase grain production and the potato yield, the nation's meat supply was not damaged. Rather than implement wholesale changes in land use in response to demand and high grain prices, farmers adapted to new market conditions and, through the use of turnip husbandry, were able to increase both the grain and meat supply (Macdonald, 1980). They achieved this because, as A. H. John pointed out, 'Any fall in the number of animals kept on pasture as a consequence of ploughing was ... counterbalanced by the increase in the number of animals kept on arable land', and this helped to ensure that British agriculture was not seriously unbalanced at the end of the war (John, 1967: 38). At one level, the overall success of British farmers may be measured by the general improvements which saw serious food shortages and supply problems easing considerably during the war against Napoleon, even though devastating famine did return once more in 1810–11 (Emsley, 1979: 211). At another level, it may be seen in the rise of agriculture's share of the national income from 33 per cent in 1801 to 36 per cent ten years later (Deane and Cole, 1969: 166, 291; Crouzet, 1989: 197–8).

In any assessment of the overall effect of war upon the British economy, much depends upon how broadly the context is set. More often than not, that context has been provided by discussion of the course and form taken by Britain's 'industrial revolution'.

With regard to this, war cannot be said to have had any dramatic catalytic effects upon the process of industrialisation, yet neither did it serve greatly to retard industrial development. Moving beyond the industrial sector, however, it becomes clear that war was of the greatest importance to the long-term strengthening of Britain's economy, most notably through the part it played in facilitating the expansion of empire and the rise of London as the world's leading financial centre. Indeed, as far as trade, commerce and financial services were concerned, wars against France enabled Britain markedly to improve its competitive standing in the world (O'Brien, 1989a: 368–72; Crouzet, 1964). In view of this, Britain's military performance must be judged as all the more remarkable. Ultimate victory against France was achieved without seriously weakening the nation's broad capacity to sustain, in the long run, the various processes associated with industrialisation and broader economic improvement. Rates of growth might well have been modest between 1790 and 1820, but Britain was still able to emerge from twenty years of war reasonably well placed to take advantage of a lengthy period of uninterrupted peace. Instead of concluding that eighteenth-century Britain was unable to fight successful large-scale wars *and* sustain reasonable rates of growth, it is perhaps more appropriate to draw attention to the fact that Britain was able to commit huge resources to the struggle against France without suffering too many damaging economic consequences in the long term.

Afterword

Britain was a nation at war for much of the time between 1688 and 1815, yet it is only in recent years that the full implications of this state of affairs have been acknowledged and explored by historians, and it is only now that we are beginning more fully to understand the importance and consequences of developments on the home front. The domestic history of war in this period might have far less colour, dash, and vigour about it than accounts of military and naval exploits in Europe and further afield, but it is no less important in helping to explain Britain's long-term success and rise to a position of ascendancy among the great powers. In countless different ways, the victories secured by the army and navy were dependent upon the routine and often barely acknowledged efforts of thousands of anonymous men and women who toiled in the shipyard, armoury, foundry, field, and government office to provide the sustained level of support that was necessary for the successful prosecution of extended wars of attrition. Moreover, for most of the time, those who remained at home offered the patriotic and loyal support that was necessary for successive war efforts to be undertaken in the face of acute economic and social strain.

As British society and the economy gradually attuned itself to the demands of war, Britons grew accustomed to wartime conditions and the state became increasingly adept at meeting the various challenges posed to it by France. In all areas of war-related endeavour, processes of trial and error, the development of new methods and techniques, and the borrowing of ideas from others allowed ministers and officials to establish systems and procedures which, over time, became refined, reliable, tried, and trusted. Of course, this favourable long-term outcome masks the fact that

Britain often owed her survival and the relative stability of the home front more to luck than judgement. Not surprisingly, the general limitations imposed upon the actions of eighteenth-century governments were such that ministers always had a tendency to muddle through wars using short-term expedients and ad hoc measures rather than to develop coherent domestic policies in support of clearly defined military objectives. There was no 'war book' or master plan for them to follow; instead they relied on instincts which combined a reasonably realistic appraisal of how Britain could best conduct war with an awareness of how much financial pressure and hardship the civilian population could withstand. Most importantly, though, their economic and social policies were always formulated with well-defined political and constitutional constraints in mind. The law offered the civilian some degree of formal security against the state, and those in authority always knew that their fiscal and military measures required approval from a Parliament which retained a keen eye for any initiative which hinted at the establishment of arbitrary or 'despotic' government. Throughout all the trials and tribulations of the period, this ensured that Britain remained essentially a civilian society at war rather than a society in which, as elsewhere in Europe, civil liberties and the rights of the individual were sacrificed on the altar of national glory or survival. As a result, Britain never became, and Britons never wished Britain to become, a military or authoritarian state in which both economy and society were shaped exclusively by the need to meet the demands of war and the ongoing great-power struggle for supremacy.

Select bibliography

Place of publication is London unless otherwise stated.

Anderson, J. L. (1972) 'Aspects of the effect on the British economy of the wars against France, 1793–1815', *Australian Economic History Review*, 12, 1–20. Argues in favour of the importance of the positive effects of war upon British economic growth.

— (1974) 'A measure of the effect of British public finance, 1793–1815', *Economic History Review*, second series, 17, 610–19.

Anderson, M. S. (1989) *War and society in Europe of the old regime, 1618–1789.* A good comparative survey.

Ashton, T. S. (1951, 2nd edn.) *Iron and steel in the Industrial Revolution.* Manchester.

— (1959) *Economic fluctuations in England, 1700–1800.* Oxford. Argues unlike John (1955) that economic growth was hindered by war in a number of important ways.

Aylmer, G. E. (1980) 'From office-holding to civil service: the genesis of modern bureaucracy', *Transactions of the Royal Historical Society*, fifth series, 30, 91–108.

Baker, N. (1971) *Governments and contracts: the British Treasury and war supplies, 1775–1785.*

Baugh, D. A. (1965) *British naval administration in the age of Walpole.* Princeton, NJ. The definitive study of how the navy functioned during the first half of the eighteenth century.

— (1988a) 'Great Britain's "blue water" policy, 1689–1815', *International History Review*, 10, 33–58. Important study of the extent to which 'maritime' strategy was an extension of 'continental' strategy.

(1988b) 'Why did Britain lose command of the sea during the war for America?' in Black and Woodfine (eds.), 149–69.

(1995) 'The eighteenth century navy as a national institution' in J. R. Hill (ed.), *The Oxford illustrated history of the Royal Navy*, 120–60.

Bayly, C. A. (1989) *Imperial meridian: the British Empire and the world 1780–1830.*

Beattie, J. M. (1986) *Crime and the courts in England, 1660–1800.* Oxford. Examines the effects of war on patterns of crime.

Beckett, I. F. W. (1991) *The amateur military tradition, 1558–1945.* Manchester. Important chapters on the eighteenth-century militia.

Beckett, J. V. (1985) 'Land Tax or Excise: the levying of taxation in seventeenth- and eighteenth-century England', *English Historical Review*, 100, 285–308. Focuses on the 1690s and explains how and why governments came to rely on the Excise rather than the Land Tax for the bulk of their income.

Beckett, J. V. and Turner, M. (1990) 'Taxation and economic growth in eighteenth-century England', *Economic History Review*, second series, 43, 377–403. Important assessment of the relationship between taxation and demand within the economy.

Birch, A. (1967) *The economic history of the British iron and steel industry, 1784–1879: essays in industrial and economic history with special reference to the development of technology.*

Binney, J. E. D. (1958) *British public finance and administration, 1774–1792.* Oxford. A detailed study of the workings of government finance.

Black, J. (1985) *British foreign policy in the age of Walpole.* Edinburgh.

(1991) *A military revolution? Military change and European society, 1550–1800.* Challenges the view that a military 'revolution' occurred in Europe between 1560 and 1660 by drawing attention to important changes that occurred after 1660.

(1994a) 'Eighteenth-century warfare reconsidered', *War in History*, 1, 215–33. Contests the traditional view that eighteenth-century warfare was essentially 'limited' and indecisive.

(1994b) *European warfare, 1660–1815*. Detailed expansion of the arguments outlined in Black (1994a).

Black, J. and Woodfine, P. (eds.) (1988) *The British navy and the use of naval power in the eighteenth century*. Leicester.

Black, R. A. and Gilmore C. G. (1990) 'Interest rates and crowding out during Britain's Industrial Revolution', *Journal of Economic History*, 50, 109–31. Argues the case for a lagged 'crowding out' effect, with government wartime borrowing after 1793 serving to raise interest rates.

Bordo, M. D. and White, E. N. (1991) 'A tale of two currencies: British and French finance during the Napoleonic Wars', *Journal of Economic History*, 51, 303–16.

Boshedt, J. (1983) *Riots and community politics in England and Wales, 1790–1810*. Cambridge, MA. Examines various ways in which war exacerbated social tensions.

Bowen, H. V. (1993) '"The pests of human society": stockbrokers, jobbers, and speculators in mid-eighteenth-century-Britain', *History*, 78, 38–53.

(1995) 'The Bank of England during the long eighteenth century, 1694–1820' in R. Roberts and D. Kynaston (eds.), *The Bank of England: money, power, and influence, 1694–1994*, 1–18. Oxford.

Brewer, J. (1989) *The sinews of power: war, money, and the English state, 1688–1783*. An important study of Britain's development as a 'fiscal-military' state.

Brooks, C. (1974) 'Public finance and political stability: the administration of the Land Tax, 1688–1720', *Historical Journal*, 17, 281–300.

Browning, R. (1971) 'The Duke of Newcastle and the financing of the Seven Years' War', *Journal of Economic History*, 31, 344–77.

Campbell, R. (1961) *Carron Company*. Edinburgh.

Cannon, J. A. (1984) *Aristocratic century: the peerage of eighteenth-century England*. Cambridge.

Ceadel, M. (1996) *The origins of war prevention: the British peace movement and international relations, 1730–1854*. Oxford. An important study charting the development and organisation of anti-war sentiment.

Chandler, D. (1994) 'The great captain-general, 1702–1714', in Chandler (ed.), 69–91.

Chandler, D. (ed.), (1994) *The Oxford illustrated history of the British army*. Oxford. A modern, scholarly and well-illustrated survey of the army and its place in British society.

Childs, J. (1982) *Armies and warfare in Europe, 1648–1789*. Manchester. Revises the view that warfare had become 'limited' by this period.

(1994) 'The restoration army, 1660–1702' in Chandler (ed.), 48–68.

Christie, I. R. (1982) *Wars and revolutions: Britain, 1760–1815*. A good general survey with Britain's experience of war at its core.

(1984) *Stress and stability in late-eighteenth century Britain: reflections on the British avoidance of revolution*. A trenchant analysis of how Britain was able to survive a sustained period of upheaval and war.

Clapham, J. H. (1944) *The Bank of England: a history*. 2 vols. Cambridge.

Clarkson, L. A. (1989) 'The manufacture of leather', in Mingay (ed.), 466–85.

Coad, J. G. (1989) *The royal dockyards, 1690–1850: architecture and engineering works of the sailing navy*. Aldershot. A richly detailed study of the dockyards.

Cole, W. A. (1981) 'Factors in demand, 1700–1800', in Floud and McCloskey (eds.), 36–55.

Coleman, D. C. (1953) 'Naval dockyards under the later Stuarts', *Economic History Review*, second series, 6, 134–55.

Colley, L. (1992) *Britons: forging the nation, 1707–1837*. New Haven and London. An influential study which stresses the importance of war in the emergence of a British nation and sense of identity.

(1994) 'The reach of the state, the appeal of the nation: Mass arming and political culture in the Napoleonic Wars', in Stone (ed.), 165–84.

Conway, S. (1995a) 'Britain and the impact of the American War, 1775–1783', *War in History*, 2, 127–50. Argues that the economic and social impact of the war anticipated the British experience in the wars against France, 1793–1815.

(1995b) *The War of American Independence, 1775–1783*. Presents a vigorous case for regarding the war as the first 'modern' war. Good chapters on the economic and social impact of the war in Britain.

Cookson, J. E. (1982) *The friends of peace: anti-war liberalism in England, 1793–1815*. Cambridge. A detailed study of an important theme.

(1985) 'British society and the French wars, 1793–1815', *Australian Journal of Politics and History*, 31, 192–203. Examines how, in the absence of authoritarian state control, society and the nation remained unified.

(1989) 'The English Volunteer movement of the French wars, 1793–1815: some contexts', *Historical Journal*, 32, 867–91.

Cooper, R. (1982) 'William Pitt, taxation, and the needs of war', *Journal of British Studies*, 22, 94–103.

Cottrell, P. L. (1980) *Industrial finance, 1830–1914: the finance and organization of English manufacturing industry*.

Crafts, N. F. R. (1985) *British economic growth during the Industrial Revolution*. Oxford.

(1987) 'British economic growth, 1700–1850: some difficulties of interpretation', *Explorations in Economic History*, 24, 245–68.

Crimmin, P. K. (1996) 'Prisoners of war and British port communities, 1793–1815', *The Northern Mariner*, 6, 17–27. A brief study of an important yet neglected subject.

Crouzet, F. (1964) 'Wars, blockade, and economic change in Europe, 1792–1815', *Journal of Economic History*, 24, 567–88.

(1989) 'The impact of the French wars on the British economy' in Dickinson (ed.), 189–209. A balanced assessment of the economic impact of the wars against Revolutionary and Napoleonic France.

Crowhurst, P. (1977) *The defence of British trade, 1689–1815*. Folkestone. A detailed study of the convoy system and measures taken to protect British merchant shipping.

Cruickshank, D. (1985) *A guide to the Georgian buildings of Britain and Ireland*.

Davis, R. (1962) 'English foreign trade, 1700–1774', *Economic History Review*, second series, 15, 285–303.

(1962) *The rise of the English shipping industry in the seventeenth and eighteenth centuries.* Contains a useful chapter on war and the shipping industry.

(1979) *The Industrial Revolution and British overseas trade.* Leicester.

Deane, P. (1975) 'War and industrialisation' in J. M. Winter (ed.), *War and economic development: essays in memory of David Joslin*, 91–102. Cambridge. Argues that the wars against Revolutionary and Napoleonic France did little to interrupt the progress of Britain's Industrial Revolution.

Deane, P. and Cole, W. A. (1969, 2nd edn.) *British economic growth, 1688–1959.* Cambridge.

Dickinson, H. T. (1977) *Liberty and property: political ideology in eighteenth-century Britain.*

(1989) *Britain and the French Revolution, 1789–1815.*

Dickson, P. G. M. (1967) *The financial revolution in England: a study of the development of public credit, 1688–1756.* The definitive study of the way in which British public finance developed in response to the demands of war.

Dickson, P. G. M. and Sperling, J. (1971) 'War finance, 1689–1715/25' in J. S. Bromley (ed.), *New Cambridge modern history.* Vol. VI: *The rise of Great Britain and Russia, 1688–1725*, 284–315. Cambridge. A comparative study of financial developments in Britain, France, the Habsburg Empire, and the United Provinces.

Duffy, M. (1980) 'The foundations of British naval power' in Duffy (ed.), *The military revolution and the state, 1500–1800*, 49–85, Exeter. The editor's introduction offers a useful brief summary of the causes and consequences of the military revolution across Europe.

Ehrman, J. (1953) *The navy in the war of William III, 1689–97.* Cambridge. A detailed study of the navy and its support mechanisms.

Emsley, C. (1979) *British society and the French wars, 1793–1815.* A detailed chronological survey of the effects of war upon British government and society.

(1983) 'The military and popular disorder in England, 1790–1801', *Journal of the Society for Army Historical Research*, 61, 10–21 and 96–112.

(1985) 'Repression, "terror" and the rule of law in England during the decade of the French Revolution', *English Historical Review*, 100, 801–25. Examines the making and application of the repressive legislation of the 1790s.

(1989) 'The social impact of the French wars' in Dickinson (ed.), 211–27.

Evans, C. (1993) *'The labyrinth of flames': work and social conflict in early industrial Merthyr Tydfil*. Cardiff.

Flinn, M. W. (1962) *Men of iron: the Crowleys in the early iron industry*. Edinburgh.

(1974) 'Trends in real wages, 1750–1850', *Economic History Review*, second series, 27, 395–413.

Floud, R. and McCloskey, D. N. (eds.) (1981) *The economic history of Britain since 1900*. Vol. 1: *1700–1860*. Cambridge.

French, D. (1990) *The British way in warfare, 1688–2000*. Offers, through excellent detailed studies of each war of the period, a critical appraisal of the view that the British conduct of warfare was based upon the use of the navy and a reluctance to deploy troops in Europe.

Galpin, W. F. (1925) *The grain supply of England during the Napoleonic period*. New York.

Gates, D. (1994) 'The transformation of the army, 1783–1815' in Chandler (ed.), 133–59.

Glover, R. (1973) *Britain at bay: defence against Bonaparte, 1803–14*.

Gourvish, T. R. (1976) 'Flinn and real wage trends in Britain, 1750–1850: a comment', *Economic History Review*, second series, 29, 136–42.

Gradish, S. (1980) *The manning of the British navy during the Seven Years' War*. An important case study of the naval manpower problem.

Greenwood, Major (1942) 'British loss of life in the wars of 1794–1815 and in 1914–1918', *Journal of the Royal Statistical Society*, 105, 1–11. Provides an estimate of British losses.

Guy, A. J. (1985) *Economy and discipline: officership and administration in the British army, 1714–1763*. Manchester. A useful study of the organisation of the army.

(1994) 'The army of the Georges, 1714–1783', in Chandler (ed.), 92–110.

Harding, R. (1991) *Amphibious warfare in the eighteenth century: the British expedition to the West Indies, 1740–1742.* Woodbridge. A case-study of a long-range 'combined' operation.

Harris, B. (1996) '"American idols": empire, war and the middling ranks in mid-eighteenth-century Britain', *Past and Present,* 150, 111–41.

Harris, J. R. (1988) *The British iron industry, 1700–1850.*

Hattendorf, J. B. (1978) *England in the War of the Spanish Succession: a study of the English view of grand strategy, 1701–1713.* New York. The sub-title offers a better description of the contents than the main title.

Hay, D. (1982) 'War, dearth, and theft in the eighteenth century: the record of the English courts', *Past and Present,* 95, 117–60. Examines the effects of war and, in particular, demobilisation upon patterns of crime.

Hayter, T. (1978) *The army and the crowd in mid–Georgian England.* An important study of the policing functions of the army.

Heim, C. E. and Mirowski, P. (1987) 'Interest rates and crowding-out during Britain's Industrial Revolution', *Journal of Economic History,* 47, 117–39. Argues that interest rates were such that the idea that government wartime spending 'crowded out' private investment cannot be supported.

Holderness, B. A. (1989) 'Prices, productivity, and output' in Mingay (ed.), 84–189.

Hoppit, J. (1987) *Risk and failure in English business, 1700–1800.* Cambridge.

Houlding, J. A. (1981) *Fit for service: the training of the British army, 1715–1795.* Oxford. An important study, containing much more about the army than the title implies.

Hudson, P. (1992) *The Industrial Revolution.*

Hueckel, G. (1973) 'War and the British economy, 1793–1815: a general equilibrium analysis', *Explorations in Economic History,* 10, 365–96. An attempt to separate the effects of the war upon the economy from other influences, focusing in particular upon movements in relative output prices and factor supplies.

(1976) 'Relative prices and supply response in English agriculture during the Napoleonic Wars, 1793–1815', *Economic History Review,* second series, 29, 401–14.

(1981) 'Agriculture during industrialisation' in Floud and McCloskey (ed.), 182–203.

Hyde, C. K. (1977) *Technological change and the British iron industry, 1700–1870*. Princeton, NJ. Tends to play down the effect of government demand upon the output of the iron industry.

Innes, J. (1994) 'The domestic face of the military-fiscal state: government and society in eighteenth-century Britain' in Stone (ed.), 96–127. Among other things, this important paper offers an examination of the government's response to the social problems caused by war.

Jackson, R. V. (1990) 'Government expenditure and British economic growth in the eighteenth century: some problems of measurement', *Economic History Review*, second series, 43, 217–35.

Jenkins, G. H. (1987) *The foundations of modern Wales, 1642–1780*. Oxford.

John, A. H. (1955) 'War and the English economy, 1700–1763', *Economic History Review*, second series, 7, 329–44. Argues that, on the whole, war exerted a positive influence upon the economy.

(1967) 'Farming in wartime: 1793–1815' in E. L. Jones and G. L. Mingay (eds.), *Land, labour, and population in the Industrial Revolution: essays presented to J. D. Chambers*, 28–47.

Jones, D. J. V. (1973) *Before Rebecca: popular protests in Wales, 1793–1815*.

Jones, D. W. (1989) *War and economy in the age of William III and Marlborough*. Oxford. A detailed study of the effects of war upon trade and finance.

Jones, J. R. (1988) 'Limitations of British sea power in the French wars, 1689–1815', in Black and Woodfine (eds.), 33–49. Argues that the navy was not a decisive instrument of power before the second half of the eighteenth century.

Jordan, G. and Rogers, N. (1989) 'Admirals as heroes: patriotism and liberty in Hanoverian England', *Journal of British Studies*, 28, 201–24.

Joslin, D. (1960) 'London bankers in wartime, 1739–1784' in L. S. Pressnell (ed.), *Studies in the Industrial Revolution presented to T. S. Ashton*, 156–77.

Kennedy, P. M. (1976) *The rise and fall of British naval mastery*. An important study offering an overview of the development of British naval power.

Kent, H. S. K. (1973) *War and trade in northern seas: Anglo-Scandinavian economic relations in the mid-eighteenth century*. Cambridge.

Langford, P. (1976) *Modern British foreign policy: the eighteenth century*.

(1989) *A polite and commercial people: England, 1727–1783*. Oxford.

(1991) *Public life and the propertied Englishman, 1689–1798*. Oxford.

Lee, C. H. (1986) *The British economy since 1700: a macroeconomic perspective*. Cambridge.

Lloyd, C. (1968) *The British seaman, 1200–1860: a social survey*. Plenty of descriptive detail on recruitment and the manning problem.

Longmate, N. (1991) *Island fortress: the defence of Great Britain, 1603–1945*.

Lovell, M. C. (1957) 'The Bank of England as lender of last resort in the crises of the eighteenth century', *Explorations in Entrepreneurial History*, 10, 8–21.

Macdonald, S. (1980) 'Agricultural responses to a changing market during the Napoleonic Wars', *Economic History Review*, second series, 33, 59–71.

Macleod, C. (1988) *Inventing the Industrial Revolution: the English patent system, 1660–1800*. Cambridge.

McNeill, W. H. (1983) *The pursuit of power: technology, armed force, and society since AD 1000*. Oxford. Challenges the view that military spending by the government had little effect upon the economy.

Marshall, P. J. (1992) '"Cornwallis triumphant"; war in India and the British public in the late eighteenth century', in L. Freeman, P. Hayes, and R. O'Neill (eds.), *War, strategy, and international politics: essays in honour of Sir Michael Howard*, 57–74. Oxford.

Mathias, P. (1979) 'Swords and ploughshares: the armed forces, medicine and public health in the late eighteenth century', in P. Mathias (ed.), *The transformation of England: essays in the economic and social history of England in the eighteenth century*, 265–85.

Mathias, P. and O'Brien, P. (1976) 'Taxation in England and France, 1715–1810: a comparison of the social and economic incidence of taxes collected for the central governments', *Journal of European Economic History*, 5, 601–50. Dispels the myth that the burden of taxation was lighter in Britain than it was in France during the eighteenth century.

Meyer, J. and Bromley, J. (1980) 'The second Hundred Years' War (1689–1815)' in D. Johnson, F. Crouzet and F. Bedarida (eds.), *Britain and France: ten centuries*, 139–72. Examines the long-running conflict from both the French and the British perspective.

Miller, P. N. (1994) *Defining the common good: empire, religion, and philosophy in eighteenth-century Britain*. Cambridge.

Mingay, G. E. (ed.) (1989) *The agrarian history of England and Wales*. Vol. VI: *1750–1850*. Cambridge.

Mitchell, B. R. and Deane, P. (1962) *Abstract of British historical statistics*. Cambridge.

Mokyr, J. (1987) 'Has the Industrial Revolution been crowded out? Some reflections on Crafts and Williamson', *Explorations in Economic History*, 24, 293–319. Plays down the importance of 'crowding out' in helping to keep rates of economic growth slow.

Mokyr, J. and Savin, E. (1976) 'Stagflation in historical perspective: the Napoleonic Wars revisited', *Research in Economic History*, 1, 198–259.

Morgan, K. (1993) *Bristol and the Atlantic trade in the eighteenth century*. Cambridge.

Morriss, R. (1983) *The royal dockyards during the Napoleonic War*. Leicester. Detailed study of administrative, management and technological developments in the dockyards.

Neal, L. (1990) *The rise of financial capitalism: international capital markets in the age of reason*. Cambridge. Argues in chapters on the capital markets that conditions during the Napoleonic wars assisted the British industrial revolution.

O'Brien, P. K. (1988) 'The political economy of British taxation, 1688–1815', *Economic History Review*, second series, 41, 1–32. Stresses that excises acted as the 'very foundation stone' of fiscal policy.

(1989a) 'The impact of the Revolutionary and Napoleonic War, 1793–1815, on the long run growth of the British economy', *Fernand Braudel Center Review*, 12, 335–95. A very important article which, unfortunately, is located in a rather inaccessible journal.

(1989b) 'Public finance in the wars with France, 1793–1815' in Dickinson (ed.), 165–87.

(1991) *Power with profit: the state and the economy, 1688–1815*. A brief study, presenting an overview of the how the state coped with the strains of war.

(1993) 'Political preconditions for the Industrial Revolution' in P. K. O'Brien and R. Quinault (eds.), *The Industrial Revolution and British society*, 124–55. Cambridge.

(1994, 2nd edn.) 'Central government and the economy, 1688–1815' in R. Floud and D. McCloskey (eds.), *The economic history of Britain since 1700*. Vol. 1: *1700–1860*. 205–41. Cambridge.

O'Brien, P. K. and Hunt, P. A. (1993) 'The rise of a fiscal state in England, 1485–1815', *Historical Research*, 66, 129–76. Places eighteenth-century developments in their proper long-term context.

O'Gorman, F. (1989) 'Pitt and the "Tory" reaction to the French Revolution, 1789–1815' in Dickinson (ed.), 21–37. Examines the mobilisation of wartime anti-radical sentiment.

Oxley, G. W. (1974) *Poor relief in England and Wales, 1601–1834*. Newton Abbot.

Palmer, S. H. (1978) 'Calling out the troops: the military, the law, and public order in England, 1650–1850', *Journal of the Society for Army Historical Research*, 56, 198–214. A mainly descriptive account.

Parker, G. (1988) *The military revolution: military innovation and the rise of the west, 1500–1800*. Cambridge. Offers a vigorous and persuasive challenge to Roberts's view that the military 'revolution' was narrowly located in the century after 1560.

Perren, R. (1989) 'Markets and marketing' in Mingay (ed.), 190–274.

Peters, M. (1980) *Pitt and popularity: the patriot minister and London opinion during the Seven Years' War*. Oxford.

Price, J. M. and Clemens, P. G. E. (1987) 'A revolution of scale in overseas trade: British firms in the Chesapeake trade, 1675–1775', *Journal of Economic History*, 47, 1–43.

Riden, P. (1977) 'The output of the British iron industry before 1870', *Economic History Review*, second series, 442–59.

Roberts, M. (1956) *The military revolution, 1560–1660*. Belfast. The starting point for much subsequent discussion about military developments in Europe.

Rodger, N. A. M. (1986) *The wooden world: an anatomy of the Georgian navy*. A lively detailed study which dispels many myths about life and conditions in the navy.

Rogers, H. C. B. (1977) *The British army of the eighteenth century*. A rather limited study, though not without some useful information.

Roy, I. (1987) 'The profession of arms', in William Prest (ed.) *The professions of early modern England*. 181–215.

Russell, G. (1995) *The theatres of war: performance, politics, and society, 1793–1815*. Oxford. An examination of the cultural impact of war.

Scouller, R. E. (1966) *The armies of Queen Anne*. A detailed study containing much useful information.

Seeley, J. R. (1883) *The expansion of England: two courses of lectures*.

Sherwig, J. M. (1969) *Guineas and gunpowder: British foreign aid in the wars with France, 1793–1815*. Cambridge, MA. A detailed exploration of an important subject.

Shy, J. (1965) *Toward Lexington: the role of the British army in the coming of the American Revolution*. Princeton, NJ.

Simmons, R. C. and Thomas, P. D. G. (eds.) (1982) *Proceedings and debates of the British Parliament respecting North America, 1754–1783*. Vol. I. New York.

Starkey, D. J. (1990a) *British privateering enterprise in the eighteenth century*. Exeter. A detailed study of an important aspect of the war at sea.

(1990b) 'War and the market for seafarers in Britain, 1736–1792' in L. R. Fischer and H. W. Nordvik (eds.), *Shipping and trade, 1750–1950: essays in international maritime economic history*, 25–42. Pontefract.

Stern, W. (1952) 'The first London dock boom and the growth of the West India docks', *Economica*, new series, 19, 59–77.

(1964) 'The bread crisis in Britain, 1795–6', *Economica*, new series, 31, 168–87.

Stevenson, J. (1971) 'The London "crimp" riots of 1794', *International Review of Social History*, 16, 40–58.

(1974) 'Food riots in England, 1792–1818', in R. Quinault and J. Stevenson (eds.), *Popular protest and public order: six studies in British history, 1790–1820*, 33–74.

(1992, 2nd edn.) *Popular disturbances in England, 1700–1832*.

Stone, L.(ed.) (1994) *An imperial state at war: Britain from 1689 to 1815*. An important collection of essays examining different aspects of the 'fiscal–military' state defined by John Brewer.

Storrs, C. and Scott, H. M. (1996) 'The military revolution and the European nobility, c.1600–1800', *War in History*, 3, 1–41. Stresses the extent to which the British nobility, like their European counterparts, remained deeply involved in military activity.

Straus, R. (1937) *Lloyd's: an historical sketch*.

Thomas, D. O. (ed.) (1992) *Richard Price: political writings*. Cambridge.

Thomas, R. P. and McCloskey, D. N. (1981) 'Overseas trade and empire 1700–1860', in Floud and McCloskey (eds.).

Trebilcock, C. (1969) '"Spin-off" in British economic history: armaments and industry, 1760–1914', *Economic History Review*, second series, 22, 474–90. Plays down the importance of the relationship between warfare and technological advances in general.

Turner. M. (1980) *English parliamentary enclosure: its historical geography and economic history*. Folkestone.

(1984) *Enclosures in Britain, 1750–1830*.

Ville, Simon P. (1987) *English shipowning during the Industrial Revolution: Michael Henley and son, shipowners, 1770–1830*. Manchester.

Webb, P. (1988) 'Construction, repair and maintenance in the battlefleet of the Royal Navy, 1793–1815' in Black and Woodfine (eds.), 207–19. Paints a favourable picture of the navy's building and repair programme.

Wells, R. (1986) *Insurrection: the British experience, 1795–1803*. Gloucester. Examines different forms of unrest and makes a forceful case for Britain being close to revolution during the war against France.

(1988) *Wretched faces: famine in wartime England, 1793–1800.* Gloucester. A detailed study of wartime food shortages, unrest, and the government response.

West, J. (1991) *Gunpowder, government and war in the mid-eighteenth century.*

Western, J. R. (1956) 'The Volunteer movement as an anti-revolutionary force, 1793–1801', *English Historical Review*, 71, 603–14.

(1965) *The English militia in the eighteenth century: the story of a political issue, 1660–1802.* A detailed examination of the establishment and functioning of the militia system.

Williams, J. B. (1972) *British commercial policy and trade expansion, 1750–1850.* Oxford.

Williamson, J. G. (1984) 'Why was British growth so slow during the Industrial Revolution?', *Journal of Economic History*, 44, 687–712. An important starting point for much recent debate which emphasizes the extent to which increases in government debt during wartime served to 'crowd out' private investment and retard economic growth.

Wilson, K. (1988) 'Empire, trade, and popular politics in mid-Hanoverian Britain: the case of Admiral Vernon', *Past and Present*, 121, 74–109.

(1994) 'Empire of virtue: the imperial project and Hanoverian culture, c.1720–1785: in Stone (ed.), 128–64.

(1995) *The sense of the people: politics, culture, and imperialism in England, 1715–1785.* Cambridge.

Index

New Studies in Economic and Social History

Titles in the series available from Cambridge University Press

Previously published as

Studies in Economic and Social History

Titles in the series available from the Macmillan Press Limited

Economic History Society

The Economic History Society, which numbers around 3000 members, publishes the Economic History Review four times a year (free to members) and holds an annual conference.

Enquiries about membership should be addressed to

The Assistant Secretary
Economic History Society
P O Box 70
Kingswood
Bristol
BS15 5TB

Full-time students may join at special rates.